NORMANDY
TRAVEL GUIDE 2025

Discover Coastal Villages, D-Day Landmarks, and French Countryside Charm

MONICA V. DENNI

Copyright © 2025 MONICA V. DENNI
All rights reserved.

No part of this publication may be reproduced, stored in a retrieval system, or transmitted in any form or by any means—electronic, mechanical, photocopying, recording, or otherwise—without prior written permission from the publisher, except in the case of brief quotations used in critical articles or reviews.

Table Of Contents

Introduction..10
Welcome to Normandy.. 10
Why Normandy? The Allure of Coastal Villages, D-Day Landmarks, and Rustic Charm..............12
How to Use This Guide: Your Ultimate Travel Companion....................................... 14

Chapter 1: Normandy at a Glance...............17
A Rich Tapestry of History, Culture, and Natural Beauty....................................... 17
Key Facts....................................... 18
Getting There.......................................21
Normandy's Accessibility...............................24
How to Use This Guide For Your Perfect Itinerary Builder....................................... 28

Chapter 2: Essential Tips for Travelers..... 33
Language and Customs...................................33
Currency, Tipping, and Payment Tips..............34
Local Etiquette and Cultural Insights.............. 39
Safety, Healthcare, and Emergency Contacts.. 42
Must-Have Apps for Your Normandy Journey 44

Chapter 3: The Best of Normandy's Coastal Villages... 50
Honfleur.......................................50
Étretat.......................................52
Trouville-sur-Mer... 54
Deauville.......................................56
Villerville....................................... 59

    The Secret Villages of Normandy......................61
Chapter 4: D-Day Landmarks......................66
    Introduction to D-Day and Its Impact............. 66
    Omaha Beach.. 67
    Utah Beach... 69
    Pegasus Bridge..71
    The Normandy American Cemetery................. 72
    The Juno Beach Centre................................. 75
    Personal Stories from the Front Lines.............77
Chapter 5: The French Countryside Charm... 82
    The Bessin Region... 82
    The Pays d'Auge.. 85
    Explore the Camembert Villages.......................88
    Rural Retreats... 90
    Exploring Normandy's Lush Gardens.............. 93
Chapter 6: Must-Visit Historical Sites....... 98
    Mont Saint-Michel... 98
    The Château de Caen..................................... 100
    Bayeux and Its Tapestry.................................103
    The Abbey of Saint-Wandrille.........................105
    The Medieval Town of Domfront.................... 108
    Normandy's Influence on Art..........................110
Chapter 7: Normandy's Gastronomy........ 114
    The Best of Normandy Cuisine........................114
    Apple Cider and Calvados................................117
    A Culinary Journey Through Normandy........120

Local Markets..121
Dining for Every Budget..................................123
Cooking Classes and Food Tours..................... 126

Chapter 8: Outdoor Adventures in Normandy... 129

Hiking the Normandy Coastal Path................129
Cycling Through the Pays d'Auge...................131
Sailing and Watersports on the Manche.........134
Exploring the Natural Reserves...................... 137
Normandy's Beaches..140

Chapter 9: Family-Friendly Normandy.... 145

Best Activities for Children............................. 145
Outdoor Adventures for the Family................148
Kid-Friendly Museums and Interactive Experiences.. 151
Exploring Normandy's Gardens and Parks.... 154
Normandy with Kids..157

Chapter 10: Shopping and Souvenirs....... 161

Local Crafts and Artisan Goods.......................161
Normandy's Antiques..164
The Best Shops in Honfleur, Deauville, and Bayeux..167
Exploring Normandy's Flea Markets.............. 172
A Shopper's Guide to Normandy..................... 173

Chapter 11: Normandy After Dark............176

A Taste of Normandy's Nightlife..................... 176
Theatrical Performances and Music Festivals 177

Nighttime Strolls and Historical Tours...........179

Chapter 12: Suggested Itineraries............183

3 Days: Normandy's Highlights in a Nutshell 183

7 Days: A Deep Dive into Normandy's Culture and Coastline..186

10 Days: A Perfect Blend of History, Countryside, and Seaside Relaxation............. 193

The Ultimate Normandy Road Trip............... 202

Normandy with Kids: A Family-Friendly Adventure.. 209

Chapter 13: Practical Travel Information.213

Essential French Phrases for Travelers.......... 213

Travel Insurance, Currency Exchange, and Connectivity...215

Accessibility...219

Local Festivals and Events You Shouldn't Miss... 221

Where to Get Detailed Maps...........................225

Local Tourist Information Centers.................228

Chapter 14: Beyond Normandy................232

Day Trips to the Loire Valley and Mont Saint-Michel...232

Exploring Northern Brittany......................... 236

Normandy for Art Lovers................................ 240

Conclusion...248

Reflecting on Your Normandy Journey.......... 248

Planning Your Next Adventure in France...... 250

OVERVIEW MAP OF NORMANDY

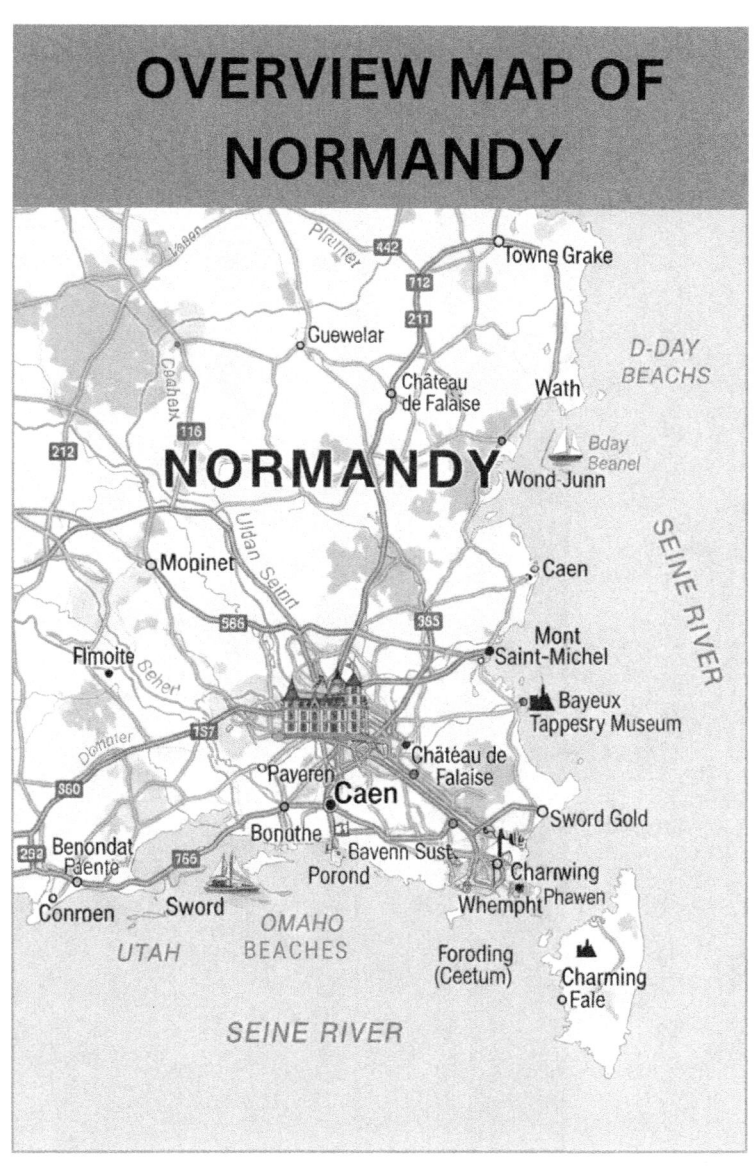

MAP OF D-DAY BEACHES

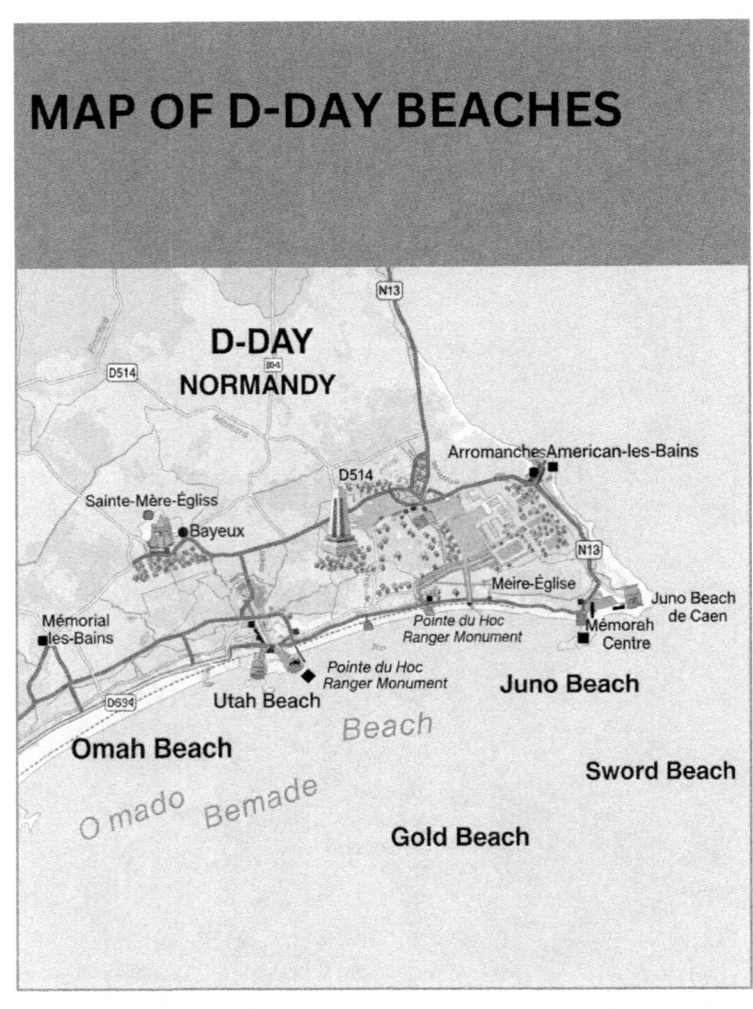

Introduction

Welcome to Normandy

When you step into Normandy, you're stepping into a landscape that tells stories—stories of resilience, beauty, and history. This northern region of France, where the English Channel meets the vast, open sky, is a place where every corner offers something unique. From the rugged cliffs of Étretat to the calm countryside dotted with apple orchards and historic towns, Normandy is an experience that blends the past and present in the most captivating ways.

Normandy's rich heritage is as much in its landscapes as it is in its landmarks. The D-Day beaches bear witness to some of the most significant events in world history, while the quiet villages and rolling hills bring a sense of serenity that's hard to find elsewhere. Whether you're strolling through Bayeux's medieval streets, marveling at the grandeur of Mont Saint-Michel, or sitting down to enjoy a glass of local CalvadosNormandy offers a journey full of discoveries. It's a place where history lives in the landscape, the people, and the way life unfolds.

As you explore this guide, you'll uncover not just the well-known sites, but also the little-known gems that make this region so special. Normandy invites you to walk in the footsteps of history, savor its culinary delights, and unwind in its tranquil corners. This book is your key to navigating one of France's most remarkable regions, a place that will leave an indelible mark on your heart.

Why Normandy? The Allure of Coastal Villages, D-Day Landmarks, and Rustic Charm

Normandy is more than just a destination; it's a region that will evoke emotions, stir your imagination, and leave you with unforgettable memories. The coastal village Normandy offers an idyllic retreat where you can escape into the charm of cobbled streets, colorful houses, and inviting cafes. From Honfleur's charming harbor to Trouville's sandy shores, these coastal towns offer an atmosphere of tranquility and authentic French living. The slow pace of life here invites you to take a moment, relax, and savor the beauty around you.

But Normandy's allure is not just its coastal serenity—it is deeply rooted in history. The D-Day landings, which took place on its shores in 1944, changed the course of the Second World War. From the American cemetery at Omaha Beach to the poignant remains at Juno BeachNormandy's World War II sites are a testament to the bravery and sacrifice of soldiers who fought for freedom. These landmarks, carefully preserved, invite reflection and provide a powerful link to the past. Walking along the sands of these beaches, you can almost hear the whispers of history, offering an opportunity to reflect on the price of liberty.

Beyond the beaches, Normandy's countryside paints a picture of rustic French life. The Pays d'Auge, with its green fields, hedgerows, and apple orchards, is as iconic as the region's Calvados and Camembert. The quiet beauty of Bessin, with its pastoral landscape, offers a peaceful retreat, while the Côte Fleurie beckons with the allure of its cliffs, beaches, and picturesque coastal villages. Normandy's charm lies not just in its scenery, but in the way that every village and every stone wall tells a story of rural French life. Here, you can sip cider at a family-run farm or explore a village market brimming with local produce—experiences that immerse you in the rhythms of daily life.

How to Use This Guide: Your Ultimate Travel Companion

This guide is designed to be your trusted companion as you explore the stunning region of Normandy. Whether you're planning a quick getaway or a long, leisurely exploration, this book will provide you with everything you need for a seamless and enjoyable trip. From historical landmarks to hidden village gems, it's packed with detailed information to make sure you don't miss a thing.

Inside, you'll find:

- **Practical Itineraries:** Tailored itineraries for trips of different lengths, so you can experience the best of Normandy, no matter how much time you have. Whether it's a weekend getaway or a week-long road trip, these itineraries will help you navigate the region with ease.
- **Local Insights:** Get recommendations from locals and experts, including the best spots for fresh seafood, quiet beaches, and where to find the region's finest cheeses and ciders.
- **Historical Context:** Normandy is steeped in history, from its medieval architecture to its D-Day landmarks. You'll find context and insider stories that bring these places to life and help you understand the significance behind every monument, battlefield, and memorial.

- **Practical Tips:** Information on local transportation, tips for navigating rural areas, where to stay, and what to eat, ensuring your travel is as smooth as possible.
- **Maps and Resources:** Where to Find Detailed Maps and Travel Tools

While this guide doesn't include physical maps, rest assured there are plenty of resources available to help you navigate Normandy with ease. Whether you prefer printed maps, mobile apps, or online resources, you'll find the tools you need to explore the region's scenic landscapes, historic landmarks, and charming villages.

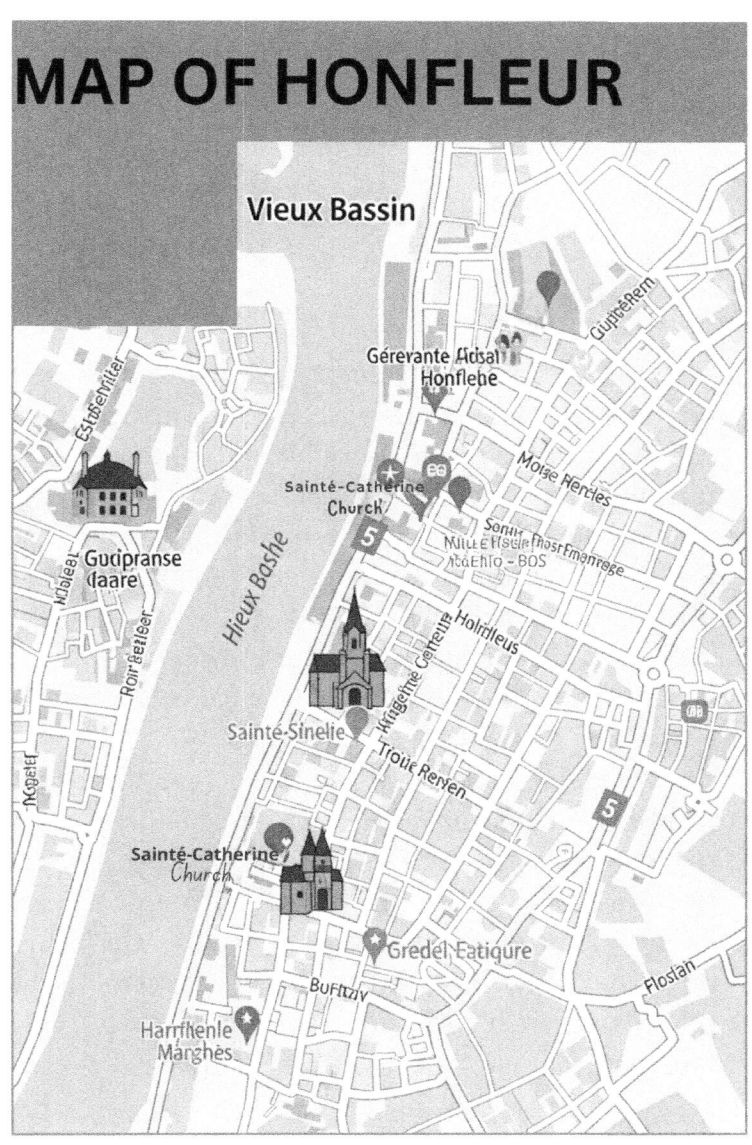

Chapter 1: Normandy at a Glance

A Rich Tapestry of History, Culture, and Natural Beauty

Normandy is a region steeped in history, culture, and natural beauty, offering something for every type of traveler. From World War II memorials to medieval abbeys and charming seaside villages, every corner of Normandy tells its own story. This land, once the heart of Viking settlements, is now a haven for those looking to explore historical landmarks, beautiful landscapes, and an authentic way of life that has been preserved for centuries.

The region's strategic location on the northern coast of France means that it has witnessed the ebb and flow of history. The D-Day beaches are just the beginning; from the imposing cliffs of Étretat, which inspired famous artists, to the rural landscapes of the Pays d'Auge, where apple orchards stretch for miles, Normandy offers a landscape that is as diverse as its history.

Culturally, the region boasts stunning Gothic churches, medieval towns, and charming villages with distinct regional cuisines, including the famous Camembert cheese, and the intoxicating Calvados apple brandy. The influence of the Impressionists can still be felt in Giverny, while Bayeux invites visitors to admire the world-renowned Bayeux Tapestry—an exquisite piece of history that dates back to the 11th century.

Yet, the heart of Normandy lies in its people—welcoming, resilient, and proud of their heritage. Whether you're dining in a quaint seaside restaurant or exploring the countryside, Normandy's blend of history, culture, and natural beauty will leave you with lasting memories.

Key Facts

Geography:
Normandy is located in the northwestern part of France, bordered by the English Channel to the north and stretching down to the rolling hills of the Pays d'Auge in the south. The region is divided into five departments: Calvados, Seine-Maritime, Eure, Orne, and Manche. Each department offers its own unique charm, from the rugged coastlines of the

Côte de Nacre to the tranquil rural beauty of the Norman countryside.

The D-Day beaches are among Normandy's most famous landmarks, while the Mont Saint-Michel, a UNESCO World Heritage Site, towers majestically over the region. The Seine River runs through the heart of Normandy, providing scenic views that are beloved by travelers, especially those exploring the Normandy Bridge or the town of Rouen.

Climate:
Normandy experiences a temperate maritime climate, with mild winters and cool summers. The region is often windy, especially near the coast, but rainfall is evenly distributed throughout the year. Spring and fall are the most popular seasons for visiting, as the weather is mild, and the crowds are fewer.

- **Spring (March to May):** Mild temperatures make spring an ideal time to see flowering gardens and experience the start of the region's agricultural season, with fresh produce, including apples, making an early appearance.
- **Summer (June to August):** The most popular tourist season, with longer days and

temperatures ranging from 18°C to 25°C. The beaches become busier, especially in towns like Deauville and Trouville, but the summer months also offer the best festivals and events.
- **Fall (September to November):** Temperatures begin to cool, but the region still enjoys pleasant weather. Fall is harvest season, making it the perfect time to sample local wines and cider, and explore the apple orchards.
- **Winter (December to February):** Winter is quieter, but it offers a peaceful atmosphere for exploring Normandy's historical landmarks. Expect fewer tourists and cozy cafés with warming local dishes like potatoes au gratin and Norman stews.

Best Time to Visit:
The best time to visit Normandy largely depends on your preferences. For mild weather and fewer tourists, spring and fall are perfect. If you're interested in the region's vibrant festivals and lively atmosphere, summer is ideal, though it may come with higher crowds and accommodation prices. Winter, while cold, offers a quieter, more reflective experience for those seeking solitude or interested in off-season prices.

Getting There

By Air:
- Caen Carpiquet Airport (CFR) is the main regional airport serving Normandy, located just outside the city of Caen. It offers flights to and from major French cities and some international destinations.
- Rouen Airport and Deauville Normandy Airport are also convenient choices for those flying into the region. Deauville is particularly popular for travelers heading to the Côte Fleurie area, known for its glamorous beach resorts.
- Paris Charles de Gaulle Airport (CDG) is another major international gateway to Normandy. From Paris, it's about a 2 to 3-hour drive to the Normandy coast or you can take a train from Gare Saint-Lazare to Rouen or Caen.

By Train:
Trains are one of the best ways to travel around Normandy. The Paris to Caen route takes approximately 2 hours, while the Paris to Rouen train takes about 1.5 hours. Once in Normandy, regional trains run frequently to towns and cities across the region, including Le Havre, Bayeux, and

Cherbourg. Consider purchasing a Normandy Pass for discounted train tickets if you plan to travel extensively within the region.

By Car:
If you prefer the flexibility of driving, renting a car is a great way to explore the region. Normandy is well-connected by highways, with the A13 and A84 offering easy access to most destinations. A car gives you the freedom to explore the D-Day beaches, apple orchards, and hidden coastal villages at your own pace. However, be aware that rural areas may have winding roads and limited parking in small towns, so plan ahead.

By Bus:
There are also intercity bus services available between major cities in Normandy and Paris, providing affordable options for travelers. These are particularly useful for those on a budget, but travel times can be longer compared to trains or cars.

Getting Around Locally:
Once in Normandy, public transportation is reliable but not as frequent in the rural areas. If you plan to visit smaller villages or the countryside, renting a car or using local taxis is recommended. Alternatively, cycling is a popular option for

exploring Normandy's countryside, with several dedicated bike paths connecting coastal and inland towns.

Travel Tips:

- **Plan Ahead:** Especially during the high season (summer), it's wise to book accommodations and transport in advance to avoid disappointment.
- **Local Tourism Offices:** Don't forget to stop by the local tourism offices to get the latest information on events, exhibitions, and hidden gems.
- **Language:** While many people in the tourism industry speak English, knowing a few basic French phrases will enrich your experience. For instance, "Bonjour" (Hello) and "Merci" (Thank you) go a long way in making connections with locals.
- **Stay Flexible:** Normandy has much to offer off the beaten path, so allow room for spontaneous adventures in this ever-inviting region.

Normandy's Accessibility

Normandy is a region that welcomes everyone, offering accessible travel options that cater to people of all abilities. From wheelchair-friendly accommodations to accessible transportationThere are plenty of options to ensure that everyone can enjoy the beauty, history, and culture of this remarkable region.

1. Accessible Accommodation:
Most towns and cities in Normandy are equipped with hotels, guesthouses, and rentals that prioritize accessibility. For example:

- Deauville and Caen offer a variety of wheelchair-accessible hotels with ramps, wide doors, and bathrooms designed for easy access.
- Rouen has several accommodations with accessible facilities, including low-bed accommodations and roll-in showers. Many of these are available for booking through platforms like Booking.com or Airbnb, where accessibility features are clearly marked.

For those seeking more specialized options, the Tourism Office in many Normandy towns can provide recommendations for accommodations tailored to your needs.

2. Accessible Transportation:
Traveling through Normandy is relatively easy, even for those with limited mobility. Here's a breakdown of accessible transport options:

- **Trains:** The French SNCF (National Rail) network provides accessible services for passengers with disabilities, including spaces for wheelchairs and assistance at major train stations. Be sure to book your assistance in advance through SNCF's official website or via their dedicated hotline.
- **Buses:** Many regional buses in Normandy are accessible to those with reduced mobility, with low floors, ramps, and spaces for wheelchairs. Le Havre, Caen, and Rouen have especially accessible local transport systems, making it easy to navigate the city centers.
- **Taxis and Ride-Sharing:** Accessible taxis with ramps are available in most cities, and ride-sharing services like Uber also offer vehicles that can accommodate wheelchairs. It's best to confirm accessibility needs when booking in advance.

3. Attractions for All:
Normandy's historical and natural sites are committed to being accessible:

- **Mont Saint-Michel:** While the abbey itself has some steep paths, the lower levels of Mont Saint-Michel are accessible, with ramps and elevators available at certain points. The shuttle buses to the island are also wheelchair accessible.
- **D-Day Beaches:** Many of the D-Day memorials are equipped with wheelchair-accessible paths. The Normandy American Cemetery at Omaha Beach has paved walkways and designated wheelchair spaces for visitors. Other memorials, like Juno Beach Centre, also provide accessible pathways and facilities.
- **Museums and Galleries:** The Bayeux Tapestry Museum, Musée de la Tapisserie de Bayeux, and Caen Memorial Museum all offer wheelchair access and special services like audio guides and sign language interpreters. Be sure to check with the museums in advance for any specific accessibility needs.

4. Accessible Outdoor Experiences:
Normandy's outdoor activities are equally inclusive:

- **Nature Reserves:** Normandy offers a range of accessible nature reserves and parks, such as the Parc Naturel Régional des Boucles de la Seine and the Pays de Bray, both of which have accessible walking trails and paths suitable for wheelchairs.
- **Cycling:** Normandy is known for its beautiful cycling routes, and many of these paths are wheelchair accessible or can be navigated with specialized adaptive bikes. For example, the Le Vélo Francette route is popular among cyclists, and some areas provide adapted bike rentals for those with disabilities.

How to Use This Guide For Your Perfect Itinerary Builder

This travel guide has been designed not just to provide recommendations, but to be a tool that helps you create a tailored itinerary to suit your travel preferences, whether you're visiting for a weekend getaway or a more extended stay in Normandy. Here's how you can use this guide to plan your ideal trip:

1. Tailored Itineraries for Every Traveler:
Throughout the guide, you'll find suggested itineraries based on time and interests. Whether you have just a few days or a full week, these itineraries will help you make the most of your time. Each itinerary includes recommendations for must-see landmarks, hidden gems, and even local food experiences to ensure you experience the best of Normandy.

- **Short Stay Itinerary (3 Days):** For those with limited time, we've crafted a quick, yet comprehensive, three-day itinerary that covers the key sights, including D-Day beaches, Bayeux, and the Normandy coast.
- **Extended Stay Itinerary (7-10 Days):** If you have more time, our seven-day itinerary allows you to explore more deeply, including the apple orchards of Pays d'Auge, Norman castles, and the stunning Côte Fleurie.
- **Special Interest Itinerary:** Whether you're into history, nature, or food, we've provided detailed itineraries focused on specific themes. Follow the D-Day legacy route, or dive into Normandy's gastronomic delights, or even the Impressionist art trail.

2. Interactive Planning Tools:
We've designed this guide to be more than just a list of destinations. Use the information in each chapter to plan your route, decide on your accommodation, and choose your activities for the day. At the beginning of each chapter, you'll find a short summary of what the chapter covers, followed by specific recommendations on what to do and see in each location.

- **Day-by-Day Breakdown:** Each itinerary is broken down into manageable chunks, allowing you to follow along each day and check off the sites you've visited. The days are paced to ensure you don't feel rushed, but also to help you maximize your time in the region.
- **Personalized Recommendations:** Based on your preferences, you can skip the more crowded tourist spots in favor of hidden gems or local favorites. Want to explore Normandy's lesser-known coastal towns or discover a local café in Honfleur? It's all included in the guide, allowing for more flexibility.

3. Insider Tips for a Personalized Experience:

Throughout this guide, we've added insider tips from locals and frequent travelers to Normandy. These aren't just typical tourist recommendations but valuable insights that will make your experience much more personal and enjoyable.

- **Local Recommendations:** Whether it's the best place to catch the sunset over the Côte de Nacre or where to find the freshest seafood in Honfleur, these tips will help you find the places only the locals know.
- **Timing Your Visit:** Learn the best times of day to visit popular attractions to avoid crowds, and discover hidden gems that offer a quieter, more reflective experience.

By following these tips and using the suggested itineraries, you'll create a personalized, seamless, and rewarding experience in Normandy—whether it's your first time here or your tenth. This guide is meant to be more than just a travel book; it's your companion in planning a trip that's as unique as you are.

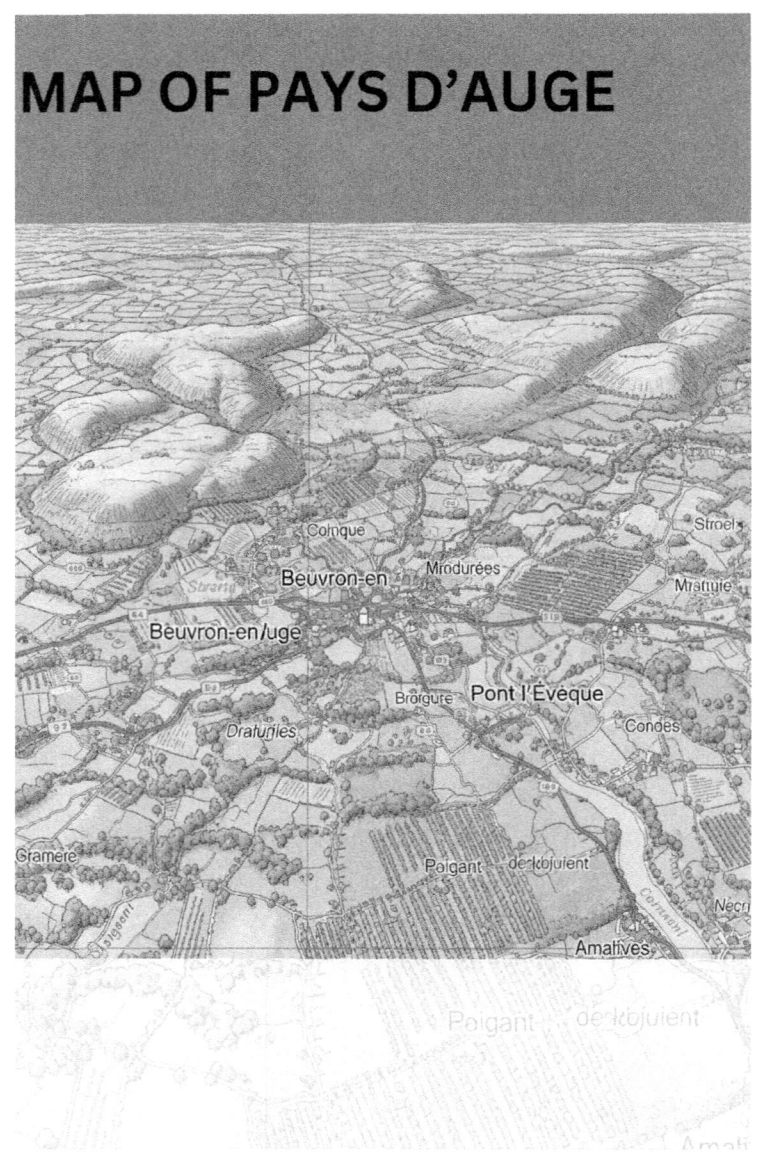

Chapter 2: Essential Tips for Travelers

Language and Customs

When traveling to Normandy, it's important to embrace the local language and customs to enrich your experience. While many people working in tourist areas speak English, especially in cities like Caen and Rouen, having a basic understanding of French will go a long way in making your trip more enjoyable and respectful to the local culture.

Language Tips:
- French is the official language in Normandy, and while younger people and those in the tourism industry often speak English, speaking a few words of French can help build rapport with locals and show respect for their culture.

Here are some basic French phrases that will serve you well:

- Bonjour (Good morning)
- Merci (Thank you)

- S'il vous plaît (Please)
- Excusez-moi (Excuse me)
- Parlez-vous anglais? (Do you speak English?)
- Où est…? (Where is…?)
- Combien ça coûte? (How much does it cost?)

Insider Tip: The French are proud of their language, so even if your French isn't perfect, locals will appreciate the effort. A polite greeting in French, such as "Bonjour" when entering shops or restaurants, is always appreciated.

Currency, Tipping, and Payment Tips

Currency:
- Euro (€) is the official currency used in Normandy, as in the rest of France. Credit cards are widely accepted in most restaurants, shops, and hotels, especially in larger towns like Caen or Rouen. However, smaller towns and more rural areas may still prefer cash for small transactions, so it's always a good idea to carry some cash.

Insider Tip: Currency exchange is straightforward at the local banks, ATMs, or currency exchange offices. Most ATMs in France have no additional fee for international withdrawals, but check with your bank before traveling to avoid high exchange rates or foreign transaction fees.

Tipping:

- **Restaurants:** Tipping is not compulsory in France, as service charges are included in your bill. However, it's appreciated to leave a small tip of about 5-10% if the service has been exceptional. For example, if your bill is €30, leaving around €2-3 is a nice gesture.
- **Taxis:** Tipping is not required, but rounding up the fare to the nearest €1 or €2 is customary for good service.
- **Hotels:** For hotel staff, leaving a small tip of €1-2 per night for housekeepers is a kind gesture. Porters generally expect €1-2 per bag.

Payment Methods:

- **Credit Cards:** Most businesses in Normandy accept major credit cards like Visa, MasterCard, and American Express. However, be aware that some small businesses, especially in more rural areas, may only accept cash or charge a fee for card payments under a certain amount.

- **Mobile Payments:** Apple Pay and Google Pay are accepted in many establishments, particularly in urban areas. Contactless payments are increasingly popular and convenient for small transactions, such as in cafes or shops.

Insider Tip: Some small vendors and markets may not accept credit cards. Carrying small denominations of cash can help you make small purchases in these situations, especially when buying from local artisans or farmers' markets.

Taxes and Refunds:
- VAT (Value Added Tax) is included in the price of goods and services in France. The standard rate is 20%, but some items such as books or food products may be taxed at a lower rate.
- **Tax Refunds:** If you're a non-EU resident and spend over €100 in one store, you are eligible for a VAT refund at the airport. Ask for a tax-free shopping form when you make a purchase, and you can get a portion of the tax refunded when you leave the EU.

Pro Tips:

- **SIM Cards and Connectivity:** If you plan to use your phone while in Normandy, consider purchasing a French SIM card. This will save you from expensive roaming charges and ensure that you can easily access maps, translation apps, and your hotel information. Many service providers offer short-term plans for tourists.

- **Language Apps:** For those who don't speak French fluently, apps like Google Translate or Duolingo can be invaluable. Many French people are patient and appreciative of the effort to communicate, even if it's with a little help from technology.

- **Stay Alert with Scams:** While Normandy is a relatively safe place, be cautious of common tourist scams, particularly in crowded areas like Rouen or Deauville. Always be aware of your surroundings and keep your belongings secure.

By understanding the local language, customs, currency practices, and payment systems, your experience in Normandy will be much more enjoyable and stress-free. Embrace the local culture, and the people will likely reciprocate with a warm welcome, making your time in this beautiful region even more memorable.

Local Etiquette and Cultural Insights

When traveling to Normandy, it's essential to be aware of local customs and cultural practices that will enhance your experience and show respect for the people and traditions of the region. Normans take pride in their rich heritage, and understanding their etiquette will allow you to blend in more easily and enjoy a warmer reception from locals.

1. Greetings and Conversation:
- Greetings in France are essential, and Bonjour (Good Morning) is the standard way

to say hello. It is polite to greet shopkeepers, restaurant staff, and anyone you interact with throughout the day.
- When meeting new people, a firm handshake is the most common greeting, and among close friends or acquaintances, "la bise" (the cheek kiss) may be exchanged. However, la bise is generally reserved for people you know well, so a handshake is always safer.

2. Dining Etiquette:
- Dining is an important part of French culture, and meals are considered a time to socialize and enjoy food.
- Keep your hands on the table, but not your elbows. It's considered polite to keep your hands visible but not to place them on your lap.
- **Wait for the host to begin:** In more formal settings, the host will often start the meal before anyone else begins eating. In casual settings, it's polite to wait until everyone has been served.
- **Complimenting the Chef:** In Normandy, meals are a source of pride, especially local specialties like Camembert cheese or Calvados cider. If you enjoy the meal, it's

always appreciated to give a compliment to the chef or waiter. You may say, "C'était délicieux!" (It was delicious!).

3. Dress Code and Appearance:
- While Normandy is relaxed in many ways, smart casual attire is preferred for dining and cultural events. Locals tend to dress neatly, and if you're visiting more upscale restaurants or attending a cultural event, opt for something a bit more formal.

If you're exploring smaller villages or countryside areas, comfortable shoes are a must as you might encounter cobbled streets or uneven terrain.

4. Punctuality:
- Punctuality is valued, especially for business meetings or formal events. If you are invited to someone's home for dinner, it's polite to arrive on time or just slightly early.
- In casual settings, arriving 10-15 minutes late is usually acceptable, but it's best to let the host know if you're running behind.

5. Tipping:
- While tipping is not mandatory in France, leaving a small tip for good service is appreciated. This can range from rounding

up the bill to leaving a 5-10% gratuity in restaurants.

Safety, Healthcare, and Emergency Contacts

1. Safety in Normandy:

Normandy is known for being a relatively safe destination for tourists. Violent crime is rare, and petty theft (such as pickpocketing) is not a significant concern, though it's always wise to be cautious in crowded areas or tourist hotspots.

- **Pickpocketing:** While Normandy is generally safe, be mindful of your belongings in more crowded places like Rouen or Deauville, especially in busy markets or transportation hubs.
- **Street Safety:** In rural areas, roads can be narrow, so be cautious when walking near busy streets or along the coast.

2. Healthcare in Normandy:

- **Healthcare system:** France has one of the best healthcare systems in the world, and tourists are able to receive high-quality care. EU citizens can use their European Health Insurance Card (EHIC) for medical treatment, while non-EU citizens are advised

to have travel insurance that covers health costs.
- **Pharmacies:** Pharmacies are common in most towns, and you'll easily find one in case you need medication. If you require prescription medicine, bring the necessary paperwork and a copy of the prescription with you, as some medications may not be available over the counter.

3. Emergency Contacts:

- **Emergency Services:** The emergency number for police is 17, for medical emergencies is 15, and for fire emergencies is 18.
- **English-speaking medical services:** Some hospitals and clinics in Normandy, especially in cities like Rouen and Caen, offer English-speaking services. However, in rural areas, it's best to have someone who speaks French assist you in case of a medical issue.

4. Pharmacies and Hospitals:

- Pharmacies (Pharmacie) are widely available in towns and cities. In case of a medical issue, a local pharmacy can assist with over-the-counter remedies and advice. Look

for a green cross symbol to identify pharmacies.
- **Hospitals and clinics:** Major cities like Rouen, Caen, and Le Havre have hospitals with emergency rooms. If you're in a more rural area, you may need to go to the nearest town to access a health center (Centre de Santé).

Must-Have Apps for Your Normandy Journey

To make your trip to Normandy smoother and more enjoyable, here are some essential mobile apps that will help you navigate the region, discover hidden gems, and plan your days more efficiently.

1. Google Maps (Navigation and Directions)
- Google Maps is indispensable for navigating Normandy, whether you're driving, walking, or cycling. It offers turn-by-turn directions, real-time traffic updates, and walking routes for historic towns and nature reserves. Download offline maps ahead of time if you're going to rural areas with poor signal coverage.

2. SNCF (Train Travel)
- If you plan on traveling by train, the SNCF app is a must-have. It offers schedules, ticket purchases, and real-time updates for all trains in France, including the regional lines connecting Normandy's towns and cities. You can book your train tickets and see seat availability directly from the app.

3. Normandy Tourisme (Local Guide)
- This app, available for both Android and iOS, is perfect for discovering what's going on in Normandy during your visit. It provides details on local attractions, events, and festivals in real-time. Whether you're looking for a local market or a hidden vineyard, Normandy Tourisme is your go-to guide for up-to-date travel information.

4. Citymapper (Public Transport)
- For getting around Rouen, Caen, or Le Havre, Citymapper is an excellent app for navigating public transportation systems. It provides information on buses, trams, and the metro, with real-time updates and easy-to-follow maps.

5. TripAdvisor (Attractions and Reviews)
- For reviews and recommendations on restaurants, attractions, and hotels, TripAdvisor is the go-to app for unbiased feedback from fellow travelers. It's especially useful for finding local dining gems, hidden attractions, and off-the-beaten-path experiences.

6. Yelp (Dining and Services)
- If you're looking for the best local restaurants or services in Normandy, Yelp will point you in the right direction. Whether it's a seafood restaurant along the Côte Fleurie or a cozy café in Bayeux, Yelp has reviews and ratings to help you make informed decisions.

7. TheFork (Restaurant Reservations)
- Booking a table in Normandy's best restaurants is made easy with TheFork. The app allows you to reserve tables at top-rated restaurants in Rouen, Deauville, and beyond. You can also find special deals and discounts for dining.

8. XE Currency (Currency Converter)
- To keep track of exchange rates, XE Currency offers live rates and a handy currency converter. It's a useful tool for managing your budget while traveling, especially if you're not familiar with the Euro's fluctuations.

By using these must-have apps, you can easily plan your days in Normandy, find the best attractions, and make your experience as seamless and enjoyable as possible. The convenience of having everything in one place will allow you to focus on what matters most—enjoying your time in this beautiful region.

MAP OF CAMEMBERT VILLAGE

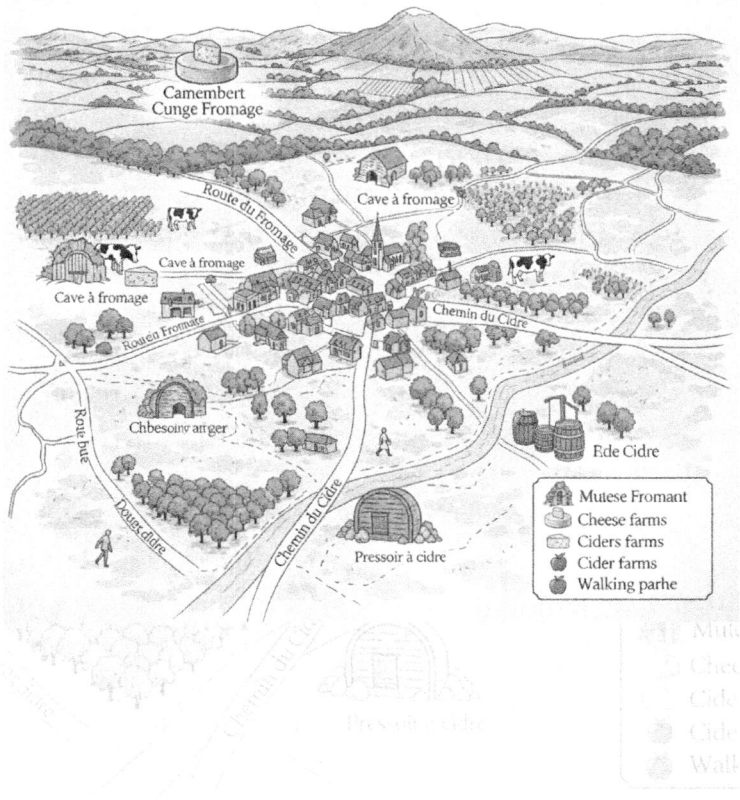

Chapter 3: The Best of Normandy's Coastal Villages

Honfleur

Nestled along the Seine Estuary, Honfleur is one of Normandy's most charming and historically rich towns, offering a perfect blend of natural beauty and artistic heritage. The town is renowned for its picturesque harbor, where colorful fishing boats bob gently in the water, surrounded by cobblestone streets and historic buildings that have inspired artists for centuries.

1. The Vieux Bassin (Old Harbor):
The Vieux Bassin is the heart of Honfleur, where the town's famous harbor meets the surrounding narrow streets. Here, you'll find old wooden houses with slanted roofs that reflect the town's maritime past. The harbor is surrounded by cafés and restaurants, perfect for enjoying fresh seafood or a traditional Norman meal while watching the boats come and go. The sunset views over the water are a favorite for both locals and visitors, and the area's beauty has made it a favorite subject for artists like Claude Monet and Eugène Boudin.

2. Artistic Legacy:

Honfleur's artistic reputation stretches back to the 19th century, when it became a hub for Impressionist artists. The town was a favorite of Monet, who captured its beauty in his famous works. Le Musée Eugène Boudin is dedicated to the life and work of this artist and features many paintings of Honfleur and the surrounding landscape. The museum also holds temporary exhibitions showcasing contemporary art, making it a must-see for art lovers.

3. The Sainte-Catherine Church:

One of Honfleur's most striking landmarks is the Sainte-Catherine Church, a wooden church built in the 15th century by shipbuilders, a reflection of the town's maritime history. Its unique construction—a wooden structure with a separate bell tower—makes it an architectural marvel. The church's simple yet elegant design invites visitors to take a moment of quiet reflection amid the hustle and bustle of the town.

4. Local Markets and Festivals:

Honfleur is also known for its weekly markets, where you can find local cheeses, fresh seafood, and regional produce. The town hosts a variety of festivals throughout the year, including the Festival of Barques (the Boat Festival), celebrating its maritime heritage. If you're visiting in the summer months, be sure to check out these lively, cultural events.

Étretat

Known for its breathtaking cliffs and stunning natural scenery, Étretat is one of Normandy's most iconic coastal destinations. This small village, perched on the Alabaster Coast, has been a source of inspiration for artists, writers, and photographers for centuries. With its dramatic white chalk cliffs and the famous Arch and Needle, Étretat offers some of the most breathtaking vistas in all of France.

1. The Famous Cliffs:
The Étretat cliffs are perhaps the most recognizable natural landmark in Normandy. The Arch and Needle formations have become symbols of the region's rugged coastline. The Arch stands majestically in the sea, creating a stunning visual for anyone visiting the cliffs. You can walk along the cliffs for panoramic views of the coast, and several hiking trails lead you to different viewpoints, each offering a new perspective of this extraordinary landscape.

2. The Etretat Gardens (Jardins d'Étretat):
For a change of pace from the dramatic cliffs, the Jardins d'Étretat offers a serene and beautifully landscaped experience. Created by artist Alain Passard, the gardens feature a unique mix of contemporary art installations and classic French garden design. From the garden, you can enjoy sweeping views of the cliffs and the coastline, and the vibrant flowers and sculptures add a modern touch to the traditional beauty of Étretat.

3. The Beach and Seafront:
Étretat's pebble beach is a peaceful spot where you can relax and enjoy the scenic views of the cliffs. Though the beach is often a bit cool, it's perfect for a quiet stroll or to dip your feet in the water. The village itself is filled with charming cafés and shops selling local products like calvados, cider, and local cheeses. The peaceful atmosphere of Étretat contrasts beautifully with its striking coastal cliffs, making it a great destination for those looking to enjoy nature and the arts in equal measure.

4. Étretat's Cultural History:
Étretat has a rich cultural history that dates back to the 19th century. The town was popular with Impressionist painters, including Gustave Courbet and Eugène Boudin, who captured its unique

beauty on canvas. Today, visitors can walk in the footsteps of these great artists by exploring the areas that inspired their work.

Trouville-sur-Mer

Trouville-sur-Mer is the epitome of a classic Normandy seaside resort. Known for its sandy beaches, seafront villas, and traditional French charm, this town has been a beloved holiday destination for Parisians and visitors from around the world for more than a century.

1. The Beachfront Promenade:
The beachfront promenade of Trouville is the perfect place for a leisurely stroll, with views of the vast sandy beach, colorful beach huts, and the calm Norman coast stretching out before you. The town's beach is much larger than it might appear from the town center, and during the summer, it's the ideal spot for enjoying the sun, taking part in water sports, or relaxing on the sand. The promenade is lined with cafés and ice cream parlors, where you can enjoy a traditional French coffee or a scoop of locally made cider sorbet.

2. Historic Architecture and Villas:

One of the most charming aspects of Trouville is its seafront villas, which date back to the 19th century. The Belle Époque-style buildings with their ornate balconies and intricate details exude a sense of grandeur and nostalgia. The town itself is a beautiful mix of modern amenities and old-world charm, with streets lined by small shops, traditional bakeries, and local boutiques. Be sure to visit the Trouville Fish Market, where you can sample fresh seafood directly from the Normandy coast.

3. Casino and Nightlife:

For those looking for entertainment, Trouville's casino offers a taste of old-world glamour, where you can try your luck or enjoy a night out. The town is also known for its vibrant nightlife, with a selection of bars, restaurants, and live music venues that come alive in the evenings. Whether you're enjoying a meal at a seafront bistro or watching the sunset from a nearby bar, Trouville is the place to unwind and enjoy the lively atmosphere of the Normandy coast.

4. Family-Friendly Fun:

Trouville is an ideal destination for families. The beachfront is great for children, and there are numerous water-based activities, including sailing, stand-up paddleboarding, and kite surfing. The town also boasts a number of family-friendly accommodations, ranging from cozy guesthouses to larger resorts, many of which are just a short walk from the beach.

Deauville

Known as the "queen of the Norman beaches," Deauville is where elegance, history, and coastal charm collide. This seaside resort town on the Côte Fleurie has long been a playground for the elite, drawing visitors with its stylish villas, luxury hotels, and pristine beach. Deauville exudes a timeless sense of glamour, making it a perfect blend of relaxation and sophistication.

1. The Beach and Boardwalk:
Deauville's sandy beach stretches for several kilometers, offering both stunning views and a glamorous setting for a day by the sea. The Deauville Boardwalk, or Les Planches, is iconic, lined with beach huts decorated in vibrant colors and bearing the names of famous movie stars who've frequented the town. It's a great place for a stroll or to simply enjoy the sea breeze while taking in the spectacular views of the English Channel.

2. The Casino and Horse Racing:
For those seeking entertainment, Deauville offers a wide range of options. The town is home to a luxurious casino, where visitors can try their luck in an elegant setting. The Deauville-La Touques Racecourse is another highlight, attracting horse racing enthusiasts from around the world. The Deauville International Polo Club also adds to the town's high-society vibe, with frequent polo tournaments.

3. The Deauville American Film Festival:
Deauville has become synonymous with cinema, particularly for American films. The Deauville American Film Festival, held annually, is one of the most prestigious events in the world of cinema, attracting international stars and filmmakers. During the festival, the streets of Deauville come

alive with red carpet events, screenings, and glamorous parties. Whether you're in town for the festival or not, the town's cinematic history is felt in every corner, from the grand Cinéville Theater to the cinematic-themed boutiques.

4. Elegant Shopping and Dining:
Deauville's upscale shopping scene rivals any major European city. The town boasts a selection of high-end boutiques, featuring French and international designers. The Place Morny is particularly popular for its luxury shops. When it comes to dining, Deauville offers a variety of excellent restaurants—from Michelin-starred establishments to charming bistros. A visit to Deauville wouldn't be complete without indulging in some fresh seafood at one of its seafront restaurants.

Villerville

A short drive from Deauville, Villerville is a secluded gem that captures the essence of Normandy's charm without the hustle and bustle of the larger seaside resorts. This quaint fishing village, perched on the cliffs above the sea, offers a peaceful escape with narrow streets, rustic cottages, and unspoiled natural beauty.

1. Scenic Cliffside Views:
Villerville is renowned for its panoramic views of the English Channel. The cliffs surrounding the village provide breathtaking vistas of the coastline and the tranquil waters below. There are several hiking trails that lead through lush greenery and up to the cliffs, where you can enjoy uninterrupted views of the sea and surrounding villages.

2. Traditional Norman Architecture:
The village is a stunning example of Norman architecture, with charming half-timbered houses adorned with flowers. Walking through Villerville feels like stepping back in time, where traditional houses line the cobbled streets, and the sounds of the sea fill the air. The village is relatively small, making it ideal for a relaxing stroll, where you can take in the architecture and enjoy the peaceful atmosphere.

3. The Quiet Beach:
Unlike the busy beaches of Deauville, Villerville offers a quieter, more relaxed atmosphere. Its pebble beach is often less crowded, providing a perfect spot to enjoy a peaceful afternoon by the sea. The beach is ideal for those looking to escape

the more commercialized resorts and simply enjoy the natural beauty of the Normandy coastline.

4. Villerville's Connection to Cinema:
Villerville is also known for its cinematic history, as it was the setting for the 1962 film "Un Singe en Hiver" (A Monkey in Winter), starring Jean-Paul Belmondo and Jean Gabin. The film captured the essence of the village's quiet beauty, which has remained unchanged for decades. Today, visitors can retrace the steps of the actors and explore the locations featured in the film.

5. Dining and Local Delights:
Villerville's local cuisine is a treat for those wanting to experience Normandy's culinary offerings in a quieter, more intimate setting. Small family-run restaurants serve up fresh seafood and Norman specialties, such as tarte normande (apple tart) and Camembert cheese. It's the perfect place to savor the flavors of the region without the crowds.

The Secret Villages of Normandy

While the main towns and coastal cities of Normandy are well-known, the region is also home to a hidden world of small, charming villages that are often overlooked by tourists. These secret spots are perfect for those looking to escape the crowds and experience the authentic, peaceful side of Normandy.

1. Beuvron-en-Auge:
This small village in the Pays d'Auge region is often cited as one of the most beautiful villages in France. Beuvron-en-Auge is a timeless place, where half-timbered houses and flower-lined streets create a postcard-perfect scene. The village is famous for its cider production, and visitors can tour local cider farms to learn about the region's traditional brewing methods. The medieval market square is also home to a few quaint shops and delicious cafés.

2. Barfleur:
Located on the Cotentin Peninsula, Barfleur is a seaside village with a rich maritime heritage. This picturesque village is known for its stone houses, quaint streets, and small harbor. Barfleur is perfect for history lovers, with its 13th-century lighthouse, St. Nicholas Church, and the historic Barfleur harbor, where ships once departed for England. The village is quiet and peaceful, making it ideal for a relaxing escape.

3. Camembert:

Camembert, not to be confused with the famous cheese, is a charming village nestled in the heart of Normandy's apple orchards. The village offers a glimpse into traditional Norman life, with apple farms and cider houses dotting the landscape. Here, you can visit the Camembert Museum, which tells the story of the cheese's origins and importance to the region's economy.

4. Le Bec-Hellouin:

For those looking to explore a village with a spiritual and historical connection, Le Bec-Hellouin is a must-see. This village is home to the Abbey of Bec, one of the most significant religious sites in Normandy. The abbey dates back to the 11th century and was once one of the most important centers of learning in France. Today, visitors can explore the abbey's grounds and gardens, offering a quiet and reflective experience.

5. Saint-Céneri-le-Gérei:

Situated in the Alençon region, Saint-Céneri-le-Gérei is another hidden gem with picturesque charm. The village is surrounded by wooded hills and offers cobblestone streets and beautiful views of the Sarthe River. Saint-Céneri-le-Gérei is perfect for those seeking tranquility and natural beauty, and it has a history of inspiring artists due to its serene and unspoiled beauty.

From the glamorous resort of Deauville to the quiet village of Villerville, and the many hidden villages off the beaten path, Normandy offers a wealth of experiences waiting to be discovered.

MAP OF BAYEUX

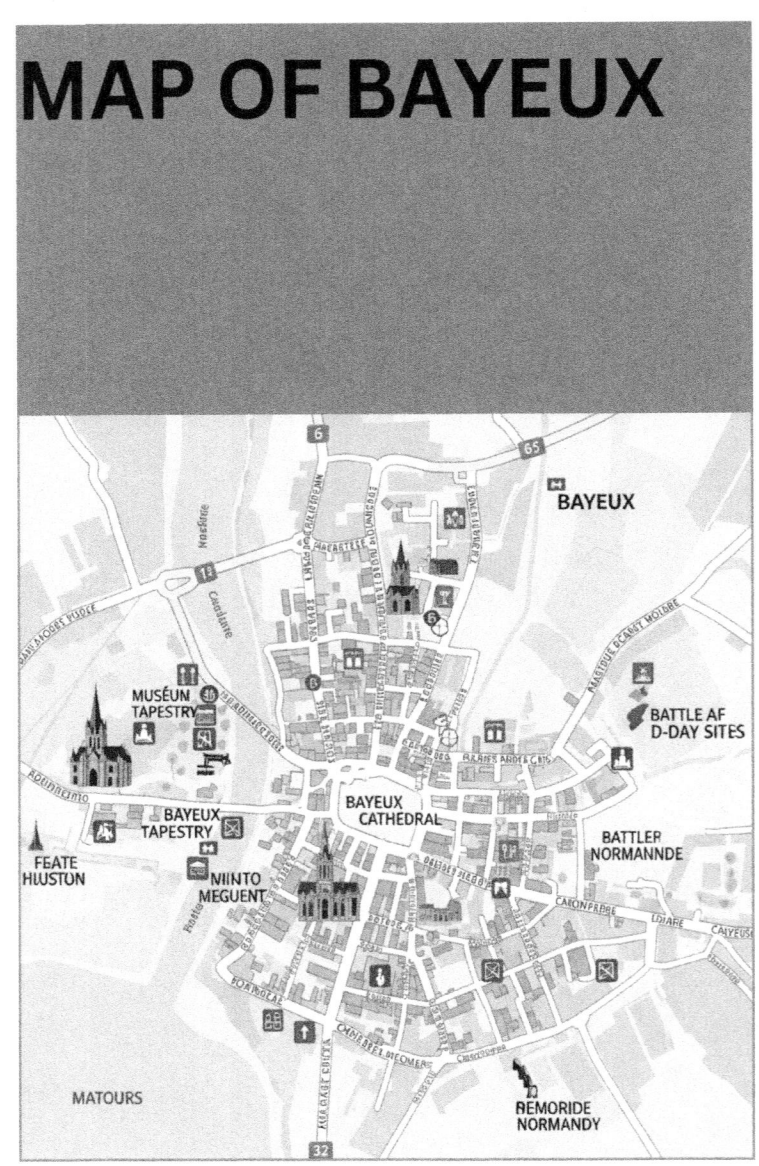

Chapter 4: D-Day Landmarks

Introduction to D-Day and Its Impact

On June 6, 1944, the shores of Normandy became the site of one of the most significant military operations in history: D-Day. The Allied invasion, codenamed Operation Overlord, marked the beginning of the end for Nazi Germany and its occupation of Western Europe. More than 156,000 American, British, and Canadian forces landed on the Normandy beaches, facing fierce resistance from the German army. What followed was a brutal campaign that eventually led to the liberation of France and the fall of Nazi rule.

The impact of D-Day goes far beyond the military victories of the day; it reshaped the European landscape, altered the course of World War II, and set the stage for the post-war world order. Today, the beaches of Normandy, along with its memorials and cemeteries, stand as solemn reminders of the sacrifice, bravery, and resilience of those who fought here.

As you visit these landmarks, it is important to understand that these sites are not just remnants of war—they are places of reflection and commemoration, where visitors can pay their respects and learn about the human cost of war. Exploring these sites gives us an opportunity to honor the lives of those who fought for freedom and peace.

Omaha Beach

Omaha Beach is one of the most iconic D-Day beaches, known for the sheer scale of the landings and the intense fighting that took place here. It is often associated with the American experience, as it was the site where U.S. forces faced some of the toughest resistance from the German forces. Over 34,000 American soldiers landed on this beach that fateful day, with over 2,000 casualties in the first few hours of the assault. The sheer bravery and sacrifice of the men who stormed this beach are what make it such a powerful place of reflection.

1. The American Cemetery at Omaha Beach:
At the far end of Omaha Beach is the Normandy American Cemetery and Memorial, one of the most moving and well-known memorials in France. This vast cemetery is the final resting place for over 9,000 American soldiers, many of whom died in the invasion or in subsequent battles. The rows of perfectly aligned white headstones, set against the backdrop of the English Channel, provide a poignant reminder of the lives lost on that historic day.

Visitors can pay their respects at the cemetery, where they can also explore the visitor center that offers exhibits on the history of D-Day, personal stories from survivors, and archival photos of the landings. The Wall of the Missing, which bears the names of the soldiers who died in the region but whose bodies were never recovered, is a particularly moving part of the memorial.

2. Omaha Beach and the Coastal Walk:
Walking along Omaha Beach is a powerful experience. While the beach today is peaceful and serene, it was once the site of intense combat. The

beach's wide stretch of sand, backed by the cliffs, was heavily fortified by the Germans, making the landings even more perilous. The Omaha Beach Memorial is located on the cliffs overlooking the beach, providing a panoramic view of the area and a deep sense of the scale of the invasion.

Visitors can take a guided tour or explore the area on their own, following the coastal walk that connects key landmarks along the beach and surrounding areas.

Utah Beach

Located to the west of Omaha Beach, Utah Beach was another crucial landing site for American forces on D-Day. While the resistance here was much lighter compared to Omaha, the landings were still fraught with danger and chaos. U.S. forces faced obstacles such as mines, barbed wire, and German artillery, but the assault was successful, paving the way for the eventual liberation of Cherbourg and the surrounding regions.

1. Utah Beach Museum:
At Utah Beach, the Utah Beach Museum is a must-visit for anyone wanting to learn more about the American experience here. The museum is housed in a former German command post and

offers extensive exhibits on the D-Day landings, the American forces who participated, and the events leading up to the invasion. Visitors can view a collection of artifacts, including uniforms, weapons, and personal items from soldiers who fought here.

One of the museum's key highlights is its display of the C-47 aircraft—the type used for paratrooper drops on D-Day—and a landing craft that is open for tours, allowing visitors to experience the kind of boat used for the beach landings.

2. The Utah Beach Memorial:
The Utah Beach Memorial stands as a tribute to the bravery of the American soldiers who fought and died here. Situated near the beach, the memorial includes statues, plaques, and a visitor center with multimedia exhibits. The memorial's location at the site of the original landings offers stunning views of the beach and the horizon.

Pegasus Bridge

While the landings at the beaches are the most well-known aspect of D-Day, the success of the invasion relied heavily on strategic objectives achieved behind enemy lines. One of the most famous and successful missions was the capture of Pegasus Bridge, located near Bénouville. This operation, carried out by the British 6th Airborne Division, was crucial to the success of D-Day.

1. The Importance of Pegasus Bridge:

The bridge itself was vital for German defense as it connected the Caen Canal to the Orne River and provided a route for reinforcements to reach the beaches. If the Germans had been able to control the bridge, it would have hampered the progress of the Allied forces. The British forces, in a daring and precise operation, landed by glider behind enemy lines in the early hours of June 6 and captured the bridge within minutes.

The capture of Pegasus Bridge was a key turning point in the invasion, as it ensured that German forces could not easily reinforce their positions at the beaches and contributed significantly to the overall success of the Normandy landings.

2. Pegasus Bridge Museum:

The Pegasus Bridge Museum is located near the bridge and offers a detailed account of the mission, complete with photos, artifacts, and personal stories of the soldiers who participated. The museum also houses a replica of the Horsa Glider, which was used in the operation, giving visitors a glimpse into the incredible bravery and precision of the mission.

Today, Pegasus Bridge stands as a symbol of the courage and determination that turned the tide of World War II. The original bridge was replaced by a new one, but the historic Pegasus Bridge is still open to visitors, offering a direct connection to the past.

The Normandy American Cemetery

The Normandy American Cemetery at Omaha Beach is one of the most iconic and moving memorials in France. Located just above the beach where thousands of American soldiers landed on June 6, 1944, the cemetery is a powerful tribute to the men who made the ultimate sacrifice during the D-Day landings and the subsequent battles of Normandy.

1. A Solemn Place of Remembrance:
The cemetery spans 172.5 acres and contains the graves of 9,386 American military dead, most of whom lost their lives during the initial assault or in the weeks following the invasion. The white marble headstones are arranged in neat, precise rows, creating an overwhelming sense of peace and reverence. The reflecting pool at the center of the cemetery adds to the solemn atmosphere, offering a

place for visitors to pause, reflect, and pay their respects.

2. The Wall of the Missing:
At the far end of the cemetery stands the Wall of the Missing, a large stone wall that bears the names of over 1,500 American soldiers whose bodies were never recovered. These soldiers, most of whom died in the days following the landings, are remembered here, their names etched into the stone as a symbol of the many who never made it home. The Wall is a poignant reminder of the human cost of the war and the countless families who were left with nothing but the memories of their loved ones.

3. The Visitor Center:
The visitor center at the Normandy American Cemetery offers a comprehensive exhibition on the history of D-Day and the American role in the liberation of Normandy. The displays feature photographs, personal items, and firsthand accounts from soldiers who fought in the region. The exhibits provide a deeper understanding of the landings, as well as the lasting impact of the American sacrifice on the outcome of the war. Interactive multimedia installations and a short documentary film help bring the history to life.

4. A Place of Reflection and Peace:
The Normandy American Cemetery is a place of not only remembrance but also reflection. The cemetery is often quiet, allowing visitors to pay their respects in a peaceful setting. The American flag flies proudly over the cemetery, symbolizing the sacrifice and valor of the soldiers who fought and died here. Visiting this sacred site offers a moment of personal reflection and a chance to honor the men who made Normandy's liberation possible.

The Juno Beach Centre

Located in Courseulles-sur-Mer, Juno Beach was the landing site for the Canadian forces on D-Day, and the Juno Beach Centre stands as a testament to their bravery and sacrifice. As one of the few museums dedicated specifically to the Canadian experience in Normandy, the Juno Beach Centre provides an in-depth look at Canada's role in the D-Day invasion and the liberation of France.

1. The Significance of Juno Beach:
On June 6, 1944, more than 21,000 Canadian soldiers landed on Juno Beach as part of the Allied invasion. Despite facing strong German resistance, the Canadians succeeded in securing the beach, allowing for the liberation of the region. The Juno

Beach Centre is located directly on the beach where the Canadian forces landed, offering a direct link to the history of the day.

2. The Museum Experience:

The Juno Beach Centre houses a variety of interactive exhibits, including artifacts, personal stories, and multimedia displays that highlight the experiences of the Canadian soldiers who participated in the invasion. Visitors can learn about the soldiers' training, the preparations for D-Day, and the personal sacrifices that were made. The museum also highlights the roles of the Canadian Navy and Air Force, whose contributions were critical to the success of the landings.

3. The Memorial Garden:

Outside the Juno Beach Centre, visitors will find a memorial garden dedicated to the Canadian soldiers who lost their lives during the invasion and the subsequent battles. The garden is a peaceful place to reflect on the courage and sacrifice of the Canadian forces, and it provides a connection to the natural beauty of the Normandy coastline. The Canadian flag flies proudly in the garden, symbolizing the lasting friendship between Canada and France.

4. Educational and Cultural Programs:
The Juno Beach Centre offers a variety of educational programs for schools and visitors. These programs provide a deeper understanding of the historical context of D-Day and the lasting impact of the Canadian forces' contribution to the liberation of Normandy. The museum also hosts cultural events and exhibitions, ensuring that the legacy of Canada's role in D-Day continues to be honored for future generations.

Personal Stories from the Front Lines

One of the most powerful ways to connect with the history of D-Day is through the personal stories of those who lived through it. The men who fought on the beaches of Normandy, as well as the civilians who witnessed the invasion, all have unique stories that provide valuable insights into the human side of war. These personal narratives help bring the history to life and offer a more intimate understanding of the bravery and sacrifice that defined D-Day.

1. Veterans' Accounts:
Many veterans of D-Day have shared their stories through oral history projects, books, and documentaries. These firsthand accounts offer a

unique perspective on the challenges of the invasion and the emotional toll it took on those involved. In Normandy, there are several memorials and museums that feature these personal stories, allowing visitors to hear directly from the men who fought here. Listening to these accounts can provide a powerful connection to the past and a deeper understanding of the courage required during those critical days.

2. The Stories of Civilians:
In addition to the stories of soldiers, the civilians who lived through D-Day also have their own experiences to share. Many locals recall the chaos and fear of the invasion, as well as the destruction that came with it. However, there are also stories of resilience, as the people of Normandy worked to support the Allied forces and assist in the liberation of their homeland. These personal accounts are often included in local museums and exhibitions, where visitors can hear from those who witnessed history firsthand.

3. Living History:
In recent years, there has been a push to collect and preserve the living history of Normandy's D-Day legacy. Veterans, their families, and local historians have worked together to create a wealth of material

that ensures the story of D-Day will never be forgotten. Many of these stories are available at the Normandy Memorials, including Omaha Beach, Juno Beach, and Pegasus Bridge, where visitors can explore personal stories through interactive displays and audio tours.

4. The Legacy of D-Day:
The legacy of D-Day is not just in the monuments, memorials, and cemeteries—it's in the people who lived through it and the families who continue to honor their ancestors' sacrifices. The stories of those who participated in the landings, both military and civilian, are a reminder that D-Day was a collective effort. Whether it was the soldiers who fought on the front lines or the civilians who supported them, everyone played a role in the success of the invasion.

The D-Day landmarks in Normandy offer a profound journey through history, inviting visitors to reflect on the sacrifice, bravery, and human cost of the invasion. From the Normandy American Cemetery to the Juno Beach Centre and the personal stories that continue to be told, these sites provide an opportunity to honor those who fought for freedom and to remember the events that forever changed the world. Through these landmarks and personal narratives, the legacy of D-Day endures—reminding us of the importance of remembering history and the lessons it teaches.

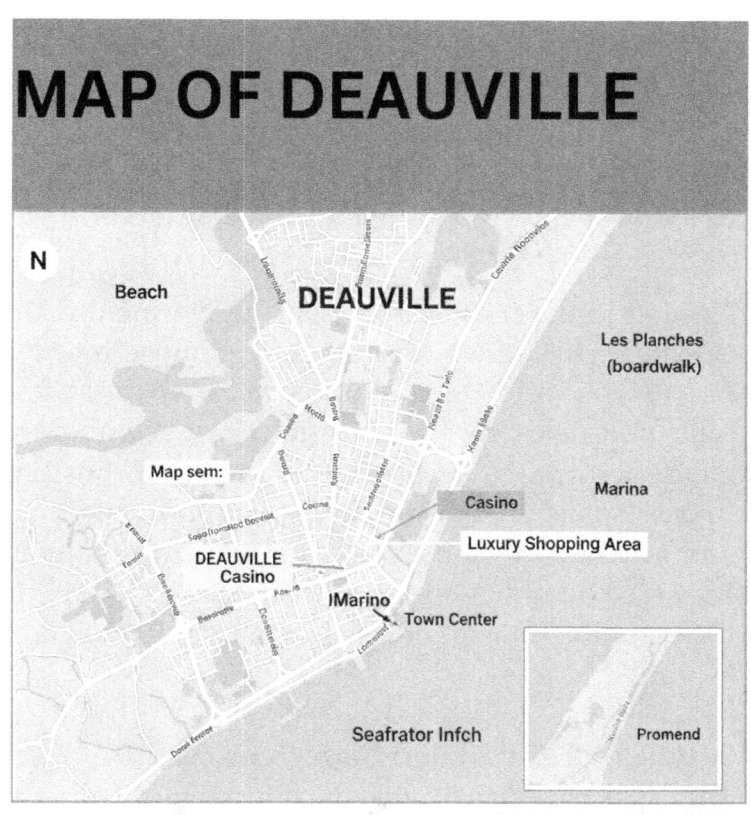

Chapter 5: The French Countryside Charm

The Bessin Region

Nestled in the northwestern part of Normandy, the Bessin region offers an authentic glimpse into the charm of rural France. This area is where rolling hills, vast fields, and countryside charm combine to create a tranquil escape from the more bustling tourist spots. Known for its agricultural traditions and proximity to some of Normandy's most famous historical landmarks, the Bessin offers visitors an opportunity to experience Normandy at its most serene.

1. Bessin's Historical Significance:
The Bessin region is deeply intertwined with the history of D-Day. Located just inland from the D-Day beaches, Bessin is home to Bayeux, a town famous for the Bayeux Tapestry, which depicts the events leading up to the Norman Conquest of England in 1066. Visitors can explore Bayeux's medieval streets, charming architecture, and ancient churches that provide a sense of the town's historical importance.

For those visiting for the D-Day experience, Bessin is also the gateway to some of the key battle sites, such as Juno Beach and the Normandy American Cemetery. Yet beyond these historical sites, the region's lush countryside remains the heart of rural Normandy, where time seems to slow down, allowing visitors to soak in the natural beauty of the land.

2. Picturesque Villages and Farms:

The villages of Bessin are quintessentially Norman, with their stone cottages, flower-filled gardens, and charming town squares. The pace of life here is relaxed and unhurried, making it the perfect spot for a slow-paced getaway. Many of the villages are dedicated to farming, and visitors can explore fields of wheat, cattle farms, and dairy farms, some of which produce local cheeses and dairy products, including the famous Camembert.

The rural atmosphere of Bessin is perfect for hiking or cycling, as winding paths lead through peaceful meadows and rolling hills. The natural beauty of the region, with its countryside vistas and tranquil settings, provides an ideal backdrop for nature lovers and those looking to escape the crowds.

3. Local Markets and Fresh Produce:
The markets of Bessin are an essential part of local life. Held in towns like Bayeux and Isigny-sur-Mer, these markets showcase the region's fresh produce, including apples, cheeses, cider, and seafood from the nearby coast. The market stalls are filled with colorful displays of local produce, creating a lively and authentic experience. Many visitors enjoy sampling the region's local specialties, such as Camembert cheese and Norman cider, straight from the producers themselves.

The Pays d'Auge

The Pays d'Auge is a region in Normandy that embodies the quintessential image of rural France. With its gentle hills, lush valleys, and endless apple orchards, the Pays d'Auge is the heart of

Normandy's cider-producing region. The area is best known for its apple-based products, especially Calvados, the iconic apple brandy of the region, as well as its famed Camembert cheese.

1. Apple Orchards and Cider Houses:
The Pays d'Auge is home to some of the finest apple orchards in France, which produce the apples used to make the region's signature cider and Calvados. These orchards stretch across the rolling hills, creating a scenic patchwork of green. Visitors can enjoy guided tours of traditional cider houses where they can learn about the production process and sample freshly pressed Norman cider.

One of the best ways to explore this region is by visiting a local cider farm. Many farms offer tasting sessions, where you can try different varieties of cider, including sweet, dry, and sparkling versions. Be sure to try Calvados, the region's celebrated apple brandy, which is aged to perfection and often served as a digestif. Some of the farms also offer tours that take you through the orchards and give you insight into the process of apple cultivation and cider making.

2. The Picture-Perfect Villages:
The Pays d'Auge is dotted with beautiful villages and charming hamlets, many of which retain their

traditional Norman architecture. Villages like Beuvron-en-Auge, Cambremer, and Pont-l'Évêque are picturesque gems, where half-timbered houses, flower-lined streets, and gabled roofs transport visitors to a bygone era. Beuvron-en-Auge, in particular, is recognized as one of the most beautiful villages in France, with its medieval buildings and cobblestone lanes.

The village of Pont-l'Évêque is known for its cheese, with the same name, which is a creamy Norman cheese produced in the area. Pont-l'Évêque and other villages in the Pays d'Auge offer the perfect blend of history, charm, and Norman culinary traditions.

3. Exploring the Countryside:
The Pays d'Auge is made for exploring on foot, by bike, or by car. The gentle hills, lush green fields, and apple orchards create a perfect backdrop for a relaxing day out. The countryside is peaceful and unspoiled, making it a wonderful destination for those looking to experience the tranquil beauty of Normandy away from the crowds.
One of the highlights of the area is the route des Calvados, a scenic drive through the heart of the Pays d'Auge, which takes you past rolling hills, apple orchards, and traditional cider farms. Along

the way, visitors can stop at charming villages, sample local produce, and enjoy the stunning countryside views.

4. Local Food and Dining:
Normandy is known for its gastronomy, and the Pays d'Auge is at the heart of the region's food culture. The area is famous for apple-based dishes, including apple tarts, Norman-style apple soups, and the ever-popular Tarte Normande (Norman apple tart). Many restaurants in the region offer locally sourced ingredients, including cheese, seafood, and meat, served alongside a glass of the local cider or Calvados.

The region's marketplaces also provide an opportunity to sample fresh local produce, including fruits, vegetables, and handmade artisan cheeses like the famous Pont-l'Évêque and Livarot cheeses.

Explore the Camembert Villages

In the heart of Normandy, the Camembert villages offer a unique and flavorful experience that celebrates the region's rich agricultural traditions, most famously represented by Camembert cheese. While the name "Camembert" is now known worldwide, its roots lie in the charming, small villages of Camembert and the surrounding region. Here, visitors can explore the origins of this iconic cheese and delve into the history, flavors, and process that make it a true Normandy treasure.

1. The Birthplace of Camembert Cheese:
The village of Camembert is the birthplace of one of France's most famous cheeses. According to legend, in 1791, a local farmer named Marie Harel perfected the cheese recipe, which has since become renowned for its creamy texture and distinctive aroma. The Camembert Museum in the village offers an in-depth look at the cheese-making process, from the milk to the aging process, and how it became an integral part of Normandy's culture.

2. Cheese and Cider Tastings:
A visit to the Camembert villages isn't complete without indulging in the local specialties. Many of the family-run farms and dairies in the region offer cheese tastings, allowing visitors to sample different varieties of Camembert and learn about the nuances that make each batch unique. These tastings are often paired with Norman cider, as the apple orchards of the region are just as renowned as the dairy farms. Local producers offer guided tours

of their farms, where you can witness the traditional techniques used to create both Camembert and cider.

3. The Perfect Pairing: Camembert and Calvados:

While Camembert is the star of the show, CalvadosNormandy's iconic apple brandy, plays an equally important role in the region's culinary offerings. Many of the farms and local cider houses offer tastings of both cider and Calvados, pairing the smooth, sweet apple flavors with the rich, creamy texture of the Camembert cheese. The combination of cheese, cider, and Calvados creates a truly authentic experience that encapsulates the flavors of Normandy.

4. The Villages and Scenic Views:

The Camembert villages are surrounded by rolling hills and lush countryside, providing a picturesque setting for your visit. The region is known for its green landscapes, apple orchards, and charming half-timbered houses. Walking through these villages gives visitors the chance to experience the region's traditional way of life, surrounded by the beauty of Normandy's rural landscape.

Rural Retreats

For those looking to immerse themselves in the natural beauty and tranquility of Normandy's countryside, the region offers a variety of rural retreats that provide comfort, charm, and a deep connection to the land. From rustic farmhouses to luxury country estatesNormandy's accommodations in the countryside allow you to escape the hustle and bustle of urban life and experience the peaceful rhythms of rural France.

1. Staying in a Traditional Norman Farmhouse:
One of the best ways to experience the authentic charm of Normandy's countryside is to stay in a traditional farmhouse. Many local farms offer bed-and-breakfast accommodations, where visitors can enjoy fresh, locally grown produce, homemade Norman cheeses, and even participate in farm activities such as apple picking or cheese making. These stays provide a cozy and rustic experience, with the added bonus of being able to witness the daily operations of the farm.

2. Country Houses and Chateaux:
For those seeking a more luxurious retreat, Normandy is home to several country houses and

chateaux set amidst rolling hills and apple orchards. These historic estates often offer upscale accommodations, including spacious rooms, gourmet dining, and private gardens. Many of these properties also feature swimming pools, spa services, and opportunities for guests to enjoy outdoor activities such as hiking, cycling, or wine tasting. Staying at a country house or chateau offers the perfect mix of relaxation and indulgence in a peaceful, picturesque setting.

3. Gîtes and Cottages:

For a more intimate and independent experience, consider renting a gîte (self-catering cottage) in the countryside. These charming cottages are scattered across Normandy and offer guests the opportunity to enjoy the peace and quiet of rural life while still being close to local attractions. Gîtes typically come fully equipped with kitchen facilities, allowing visitors to prepare their own meals using fresh, local ingredients. Whether you choose a remote stone cottage tucked away in the Norman hills or a cozy cottage near a local village, a gîte provides an authentic and flexible way to experience the region.

4. Eco-Friendly Stays:

For travelers who are conscious about sustainability, Normandy also offers several eco-friendly accommodations, including farm stays, eco-lodges, and sustainable retreats. These establishments focus on minimizing their environmental footprint, often using solar power, local materials, and organic practices to provide a comfortable stay while preserving the beauty of the surrounding countryside.

Exploring Normandy's Lush Gardens

Normandy's countryside is not only famous for its rolling hills and apple orchards but also for its lush gardens that bloom year-round with a stunning variety of flowers, plants, and trees. Exploring the gardens of Normandy is a truly tranquil experience, offering visitors the chance to enjoy the region's natural beauty while learning about its rich horticultural history.

1. Monet's Garden at Giverny:
Perhaps the most famous garden in Normandy is the one created by Claude Monet at Giverny. This iconic garden, which inspired Monet's Water Lilies series, is a must-visit for anyone with an appreciation for art and nature. The garden is divided into two sections: the flower garden, with its vibrant mix of seasonal blooms, and the water garden, with its famous ponds and Japanese bridge.

The carefully designed landscape and the interplay of colors and light provide a magical experience, as visitors can stroll through the very garden that inspired Monet's masterpieces.

2. The Jardin des Plantes in Rouen:
The Jardin des Plantes in Rouen is another beautiful garden, offering a peaceful retreat in the heart of the city. Established in the 17th century, the garden features a wide variety of plants, including medicinal herbs, flowers, and trees. Visitors can enjoy a leisurely walk through the well-maintained grounds and enjoy the tranquility of this historic garden. In spring and summer, the garden bursts into life with colorful blooms and fragrant flowers.

3. The Château de Vendeuvre Gardens:
Located in the Pays d'Auge, the Château de Vendeuvre is famous for its beautiful gardens, which combine formal and informal styles. The famous "water garden" is designed with flowing channels, water features, and reflections that create a serene atmosphere. Visitors can also explore the botanical gardens and the labyrinth of trees, which make this one of Normandy's most picturesque destinations for garden lovers.

4. The Abbey of Saint-Wandrille Gardens:
The Abbey of Saint-Wandrille, situated near the village of Fontenay, is home to a tranquil garden where visitors can experience the peaceful atmosphere of a working monastery. The gardens are designed with simplicity and beauty in mind, offering a serene space for contemplation and relaxation. The abbey's gardens provide the perfect setting for those who wish to enjoy a more meditative experience in Normandy's rural landscape.

5. Seasonal Blooms and Garden Festivals:
Normandy's gardens come to life throughout the year, with seasonal blooms marking the passage of time. Spring brings vibrant tulips and daffodils, while summer sees an explosion of roses, lavender, and sunflowers. Autumn is the time for chrysanthemums and heather, while winter showcases holly, ivy, and other evergreens. Many of the gardens in Normandy also host garden festivals, such as the Fête des Plantes at Château de Vendeuvre, where visitors can buy plants, learn about gardening, and explore new floral trends.

From the rich flavors of Camembert and cider in the villages of Normandy to the stunning gardens that define the region's rural charm, Normandy's countryside offers an abundance of experiences. Whether you're looking for a peaceful retreat, a gastronomic adventure, or an escape into nature, the heart of Normandy's countryside provides the perfect setting for an unforgettable experience.

MAP OF TROUVILLE-SUR-MER

Chapter 6: Must-Visit Historical Sites

Mont Saint-Michel

Mont Saint-Michel is perhaps one of the most iconic and recognizable landmarks in all of France. Rising dramatically from the sea, this medieval abbey and island commune is a UNESCO World Heritage site and a must-see for anyone visiting Normandy. The abbey's stunning location and centuries of history make it a symbol of faith, architecture, and natural beauty.

1. A History Carved in Stone:
Mont Saint-Michel has a rich history dating back to the 8th century when it was originally established as a monastery. Over the centuries, it grew into a fortified abbey, with walls, towers, and fortifications designed to protect it from the ever-changing tides of war and nature. The abbey's architecture reflects this evolution, blending Gothic, Romanesque, and medieval military styles.

2. The Abbey and Its Church:
The abbey itself is a magnificent structure, perched atop the island with sweeping views of the

surrounding waters. Inside, visitors can explore the abbey church, where the choir stalls and vaulted ceilings evoke a sense of awe. The mont is home to many religious artifacts, and the abbey's cloisters, with their tranquil atmosphere, offer a quiet place for reflection. Don't miss the refectory, the monks' quarters, and the salle des chevaliers (hall of the knights) that depict the life and purpose of the abbey through the ages.

3. The Tides of Time:
What makes Mont Saint-Michel even more fascinating is its relationship with the tides. At high tide, the island is surrounded by water, making it appear like a floating fortress. At low tide, visitors can walk across the vast sand flats to the island, making for an unforgettable experience. The tides, which can vary up to 14 meters, have been an essential part of the island's defense throughout history, as it could only be reached by land during certain hours of the day.

4. Mont Saint-Michel Village:
Beyond the abbey, the island is home to a quaint village with narrow, cobblestone streets, boutiques, and restaurants serving local specialties like omelettes and seafood. The ramparts offer spectacular views of the surrounding waters, and

visitors can stroll through the charming streets, exploring artisan shops and small cafés.

5. Practical Information:

- **Best Time to Visit:** Mont Saint-Michel is a popular tourist destination, so visiting early in the morning or later in the evening is ideal to avoid the crowds.
- **Accessibility:** The abbey is accessible by foot from the mainland causeway, and there are shuttle buses for visitors who wish to avoid the walk.

The Château de Caen

The Château de Caen, a massive fortress that overlooks the city of Caen, is a testament to Normandy's medieval heritage. Built by William the Conqueror in the 11th century, this fortress has played an important role in the region's military history and serves as a reminder of Normandy's significant role in European history.

1. A Fortress Built by William the Conqueror:
The Château de Caen was commissioned by William the Conqueror after his conquest of England in

1066. The castle was designed to serve as a stronghold for the Norman dukes and played a crucial role during the Hundred Years' War. The fortress is strategically positioned on a hill, offering commanding views of the surrounding city and the Orne River.

2. The Castle and Its Courtyards:
The château is vast, with impressive walls, towers, and gates that evoke the fortress' medieval past. Within the castle walls, visitors can explore the large courtyards, the keep, and the dungeons, all of which are reminders of the castle's military role. The Château also houses two important museums: the Musée de Normandie and the Musée des Beaux-Arts (Museum of Fine Arts), which showcase the region's history and art.

3. William the Conqueror's Tomb:
While in Caen, make sure to visit the Abbaye aux Hommes, the church where William the Conqueror is buried. His tomb, though simple, is an important site in the story of Normandy. The abbey and its Romanesque architecture also offer a glimpse into the early medieval church of the region.

4. The Château's Role in Modern History:
During World War II, the Château de Caen was heavily bombed by Allied forces, as the city was a key target during the Normandy invasion. After the war, the fortress was restored, and today it stands as a historical site, reminding visitors of both the medieval and modern history of the region.

5. Practical Information:

- **Best Time to Visit:** The castle is open year-round, with guided tours available to learn about its medieval history and its role during the war.
- **Accessibility:** The castle is located in the heart of Caen, making it easy to explore on foot, with nearby restaurants and shops for a convenient visit.

Bayeux and Its Tapestry

Bayeux, a charming town in Normandy, is best known for the Bayeux Tapestry, a medieval masterpiece that chronicles the events leading up to the Norman Conquest of England in 1066. The tapestry, which is nearly 230 feet long, is one of the most significant historical documents from the medieval period and is considered an extraordinary work of art.

1. The Bayeux Tapestry:
The Bayeux Tapestry is a needlework embroidery that tells the story of the Battle of Hastings and the events that led to the victory of William the Conqueror. The tapestry is an extraordinary example of medieval storytelling—each of the 58 scenes is richly detailed, offering a vivid depiction of medieval life, from battles and ship-building to the coronation of William. The tapestry is housed in the Bayeux Tapestry Museum, where visitors can view it up close and learn about its creation and significance.

2. The Town of Bayeux:
Beyond the tapestry, Bayeux is a beautiful medieval town with winding streets, half-timbered houses, and gothic architecture. Visitors can explore the Bayeux Cathedral, a magnificent example of Norman Romanesque architecture, and stroll through the town's charming market squares. Bayeux's relaxed atmosphere and historic charm make it an ideal spot to spend a day exploring.

3. Bayeux and the D-Day Landings:
Bayeux is also an important town for those exploring Normandy's D-Day landmarks. The town was one of the first to be liberated during the Normandy invasion, and the Bayeux War Cemetery, which contains the graves of over 4,000 Commonwealth soldiers, is a place of solemn remembrance.

4. The Bayeux Tapestry's Legacy:
The Bayeux Tapestry not only documents the Norman Conquest but also offers a window into the medieval world, providing rich insights into the culture, politics, and daily life of the 11th century. It's a valuable historical artifact that continues to fascinate historians, artists, and visitors alike.

5. Practical Information:

- **Best Time to Visit:** The Bayeux Tapestry Museum is open year-round, with guided tours available for a deeper understanding of the tapestry's significance.
- **Accessibility:** The town of Bayeux is easily accessible by car and train, and the museum is located within walking distance from the town center.

The Abbey of Saint-Wandrille

Nestled in the Norman countryside, the Abbey of Saint-Wandrille, also known as Saint-Wandrille Abbaye, is a hidden gem that offers visitors a peaceful retreat steeped in history. Founded in the 7th centuryThe abbey is a significant spiritual and architectural site in Normandy, combining medieval charm with a serene atmosphere that has made it a popular destination for reflection and quiet contemplation.

1. A Rich Monastic Heritage:
The Abbey of Saint-Wandrille has a rich and storied past. Originally established as a monastic community, the abbey flourished throughout the Middle Ages. It was founded by Saint Wandrille, a monk who established a monastic rule that emphasized the importance of prayer, work, and hospitality. The abbey became one of the most influential religious institutions in Normandy during the 8th century and continued to play an important role in the region's spiritual and cultural life for centuries.

Though the abbey was severely damaged during the French Revolution, it was later restored and continues to be a place of spiritual retreat and meditative silence. Today, it is run by a community of Benedictine monks, and visitors are invited to experience its calming atmosphere and stunning architecture.

2. The Architecture and Grounds:
The abbey is a beautiful example of Romanesque architecture, with its stone walls, arched doorways, and tranquil cloisters. The church is an impressive structure with vaulted ceilings and stained glass windows that provide a sense of peace and reverence. The surrounding gardens and wooded areas offer the perfect setting for visitors seeking a calming, nature-filled retreat. The abbey's medieval ambiance and secluded location make it an ideal place to escape the crowds and find a moment of stillness in the heart of Normandy.

3. Cultural and Spiritual Programs:
In addition to being a place of historical significance, the Abbey of Saint-Wandrille offers visitors the opportunity to participate in spiritual programs and attend prayer services. The abbey also organizes various cultural events, such as concerts, lectures, and art exhibitions, making it a hub of both religious devotion and artistic expression.

4. Practical Information:

Best Time to Visit: The Abbey is open year-round, but it's particularly peaceful in the off-season, when fewer tourists visit. The spring and fall offer beautiful natural surroundings, with the abbey's gardens and nearby forests coming alive with color.
Accessibility: The abbey is located near the village of Saint-Wandrille-Rançon, about 30 minutes from Rouen. There is ample parking on site, and the abbey is accessible by car.

The Medieval Town of Domfront

The town of Domfront, tucked away in the Norman countryside, offers visitors a chance to step back in time to medieval France. With its narrow, winding streets, timber-framed houses, and historic castle ruins, Domfront is one of Normandy's most charming and lesser-known medieval towns.

1. A Town Steeped in History:
Domfront dates back to the 9th century, with its origins rooted in Viking invasions and Norman expansion. The town played a key role in the medieval period as a fortified stronghold that served as a defense point during battles between the Normans and the Anglo-Saxons. Domfront's

castle was strategically important, and parts of the castle walls and towers still stand today, offering a fascinating glimpse into the town's military past.

2. The Domfront Castle:
The ruins of Domfront Castle are perhaps the most striking feature of the town. Set atop a hill, the castle offers panoramic views of the surrounding countryside and the Varenne River. Visitors can explore the castle remains, which include sections of the keep, defensive walls, and battlement. The site also provides insight into the medieval architecture and defense systems used by the Normans during the era.

3. Exploring Domfront's Medieval Streets:
The streets of Domfront are a wonderful mix of medieval charm and small-town life. As you wander through the narrow alleys, you'll encounter half-timbered houses, old stone buildings, and picturesque town squares that evoke a sense of the past. The town's churches—such as the Saint-Julien Church—are stunning examples of Norman architecture, with intricate stonework and stained-glass windows that add to the historic ambiance.

4. Local Markets and Dining:
Domfront also boasts a number of local markets and artisan shops where visitors can buy handmade crafts, local cheeses, and Norman specialties. Enjoying a meal at a traditional bistro or café allows you to experience the relaxed atmosphere of this medieval town. Don't miss sampling local cider and camembert cheese—two of Normandy's most beloved culinary products.

5. Practical Information:

- **Best Time to Visit:** Domfront is especially beautiful in the spring and summer, when the town's gardens and countryside are lush and green. The autumn months also offer stunning views, with the changing leaves creating a picturesque backdrop for the town's historic sites.
- **Accessibility:** Domfront is located about 45 minutes south of Caen and is easily accessible by car. The town is relatively small and easy to explore on foot, with ample parking available near the town center.

Normandy's Influence on Art

Normandy's stunning landscapes and rich history have inspired countless artists, from Impressionist painters like Claude Monet to contemporary artists who continue to draw from the region's beauty. The region's unique light, seascapes, and countryside have made it a magnet for creativity.

1. Claude Monet and the Birth of Impressionism:
Normandy is intrinsically linked to the Impressionist movement, thanks to the profound influence of Claude Monet. Monet was drawn to the region's unique light and natural beauty, which he captured in numerous landscape paintings. Perhaps his most famous works are those of Étretat, where he painted the cliffs and seascapes of this dramatic coastal town. Visitors to Giverny, where Monet lived for much of his life, can explore the Monet Foundation, which houses the artist's famous gardens and studio. The beauty of the water lilies, Japanese bridges, and surrounding gardens continues to inspire artists today.

2. The Legacy of Monet's Giverny:
The village of Giverny is one of Normandy's most visited destinations for art lovers. The Monet

Foundation and the gardens are a living testament to the artist's connection to nature. The gardens are beautifully maintained, offering a chance to see the very setting that inspired some of Monet's most famous works, including "Water Lilies" and "The Japanese Bridge". The town also hosts art exhibitions and workshops, allowing visitors to create their own masterpieces while soaking in the beauty that Monet once experienced.

3. Modern Artists and Normandy's Continuing Influence:
While Monet's legacy is perhaps the most famous, many modern artists continue to be drawn to Normandy's landscapes. From the beaches of D-Day to the rolling hills of the Pays d'Auge, contemporary painters, photographers, and sculptors regularly visit the region to find inspiration. Normandy's artistic scene continues to thrive, with galleries, exhibitions, and art festivals showcasing the work of both established and emerging artists.

4. Art Galleries and Museums:
Throughout Normandy, there are numerous art galleries and museums that celebrate the region's artistic heritage. The Musée des Beaux-Arts in Rouen houses works by Impressionists and

Norman artists, while the Musée Eugène Boudin in Honfleur features the works of Eugène Boudin, another key figure in the Impressionist movement. The Musée d'Art Moderne in Caen and the Musée des Impressionnismes in Giverny offer further exploration into the artistic legacy of Normandy.

From the Abbey of Saint-Wandrille and the medieval streets of Domfront to the artistic legacy of Monet, Normandy is a region that continues to inspire and captivate with its rich history and natural beauty. Whether you are visiting for the art, the architecture, or simply to explore the quiet charm of Normandy's historic sites, this region offers a wealth of experiences that will leave you with lasting memories of its cultural and historical significance.

Chapter 7: Normandy's Gastronomy

The Best of Normandy Cuisine

Normandy's culinary scene is as rich and diverse as the region itself, offering a wealth of flavors that reflect both its coastal bounty and agricultural heritage. From fresh seafood pulled straight from the English Channel to the famous Camembert cheese produced in the heart of the countryside, Normandy cuisine is a celebration of quality, tradition, and local ingredients. As you travel through the region, be sure to indulge in some of its most iconic dishes and specialties.

1. Fresh Seafood:
As a coastal region, Normandy is blessed with some of the freshest seafood in France, and fish markets in towns like Honfleur, Le Havre, and Dieppe offer an incredible selection of fresh catch. Norman oysters, particularly from the Marennes-Oléron region, are a must-try. These oysters are known for their distinctive flavor, influenced by the region's unique coastal waters.

The region's mussels, harvested from the Norman coastline, are a treat, often served in a traditional dish called moules marinières, where the shellfish are steamed in a broth of white wine, garlic, and shallots. Another classic dish is sole meunière, a simple yet flavorful fish dish made with freshly caught sole, browned in butter and lemon juice.

2. Norman Fish Stew (Cotriade):
For a heartier dish, try cotriade, a traditional fish stew from the Bessin region. This dish is made by simmering various kinds of fresh seafood, including fish, mussels, and oysters, along with vegetables, herbs, and cider. It is perfect for those looking to indulge in the coastal flavors of Normandy while experiencing a dish that has been passed down through generations.

3. Camembert Cheese:

No visit to Normandy is complete without tasting Camembert cheese, which is internationally recognized as one of France's most beloved cheeses. Camembert was first made in the village of Camembert in the late 18th century and is known for its creamy, rich texture and distinctive aroma. Many local farms in the Pays d'Auge produce their own version of Camembert, which can be sampled in traditional cheese shops or at farm-to-table restaurants.

Often, Camembert is served warm and melted, accompanied by crusty bread and fresh fruit, creating the perfect balance of flavors. The cheese pairs beautifully with a glass of Normandy cider or a splash of Calvados for an authentic Norman experience.

4. Normandy's Stews and Meat Dishes:

In addition to seafood, Normandy is also known for its hearty meat dishes, particularly those that incorporate the region's famed cider. Norman pork dishes, such as pork with cider (Porc au Cidre), are a staple of local menus, with pork belly or roast pork simmered in apple cider, creating a tender and flavorful dish. The region's duck confit and lamb stew also offer a taste of Normandy's rustic, farm-to-table cooking traditions.

5. Norman Pastries:
For dessert, indulge in some of the region's delicious pastries. The Tarte Normande (Norman apple tart) is made with local apples, often served with a layer of almond cream or a rich custard filling. Another delightful treat is the Canelé, a small fluted pastry flavored with rum and vanilla, often found in bakeries throughout the region. For those with a sweet tooth, Normandy's creamy custards and apple-based desserts will undoubtedly satisfy.

Apple Cider and Calvados

No exploration of Normandy's gastronomy is complete without diving into its famous apple-based beverages—the region is known for its cider and Calvados, both of which have become symbols of Normandy's unique terroir. These drinks, made from the region's abundant apple orchards, are woven into the fabric of Norman life and culture.

1. Normandy's Cider:
Normandy is one of the best-known producers of cider in the world, with a long tradition of apple cultivation. The region boasts a wide variety of apples, from bitter to sweet, each variety

contributing to the unique flavors of the cider. Cidre doux (sweet cider) and cidre brut (dry cider) are the two primary styles of cider produced in the region, with some variations offering sparkling options as well.

The Pays d'Auge region is particularly famous for its cider production, and visitors to local cider farms can enjoy guided tours and tastings of fresh cider straight from the barrel. A must-try is cidre fermier, which is a small-batch cider made using traditional methods. These ciders are often served in rustic wooden barrels at local bistros and pubs, and pairing a glass of cider with cheese and charcuterie is a true Norman tradition.

2. Calvados: The Norman Apple Brandy:
If cider is the drink of the day, Calvados is the drink of the night. This apple brandy has been distilled in Normandy for centuries, with the region's apples being transformed into a smooth, potent spirit. Calvados is typically served as an aperitif or digestif after a meal, but it is also used in cocktails and cooking to impart a rich, fruity flavor.

The production of Calvados is a long and careful process. Apples are first pressed into apple juice, which is then fermented and distilled into an apple brandy. The brandy is aged in oak barrels, giving it a unique flavor that reflects the terroir of the

Normandy region. The best Calvados is typically aged for at least three years, although older versions are available for connoisseurs.

Visitors can tour the Calvados distilleries in Normandy to learn about the production process and sample different varieties of this iconic spirit. Many distilleries in the Pays d'Auge and Caux regions offer tastings of Calvados, often pairing it with local cheeses to showcase the spirit's complex flavors.

3. Drinking Etiquette:
Cider and Calvados are not just beverages; they are an integral part of Normandy's cultural fabric. The French are known for their respect for local drinks, and drinking in Normandy is often accompanied by

small plates of cheese, charcuterie, or bread. If you're visiting a local cider house or distillery, expect to be offered a small glass of cider or a sip of Calvados, with an invitation to relax and enjoy the flavors of the region.

A Culinary Journey Through Normandy

Normandy's gastronomy is a true reflection of its land and history—a perfect blend of fresh, local ingredients, timeless recipes, and a deep respect for tradition. From the rich and creamy Camembert cheese to the cider and Calvados that accompany every meal, the food and drink of Normandy offer a delicious journey for the senses. Whether you're enjoying fresh seafood, savoring a slice of apple tart, or sipping a glass of Calvados, every bite and sip connects you to the heart of Normandy—its culture, its terroir, and its people.

Local Markets

One of the best ways to experience the authentic flavors of Normandy is by visiting its local markets. These bustling hubs of activity offer a wealth of fresh produce, local cheeses, seafood, and other regional specialties that reflect the true spirit of the region. Whether you're looking for handpicked apples or freshly caught oysters, the markets of Normandy are the perfect place to discover the region's culinary treasures.

1. The Markets of Rouen:
Rouen, one of Normandy's largest cities, is home to some of the best food markets in the region. The Marché des Halles is a historic indoor market that has been serving locals and visitors since the 19th century. Here, you'll find everything from local cheeses, such as Livarot and Pont-l'Évêque, to seasonal vegetables and fresh fruits. The market also features a wide selection of meats, poultry, and fish, with many vendors offering Normandy specialties like duck confit and sardines.

2. Honfleur's Seaside Market:
For those visiting Honfleur, the charming coastal town known for its picturesque harbor, the local market is a must-visit. Held several days a week in the Place Saint-Catherine, this market is known for its fresh seafood, including mussels, crab, and fish straight from the English Channel. Stalls also sell local produce, including apples, pears, and cider, as well as homemade jams and breads.

3. The Market in Caen:
Caen's market is a lively experience, especially on Saturday mornings. The market stretches through the city's historic streets, offering a vibrant selection of fresh vegetables, herbs, and local specialties. Don't miss out on the Norman cheeses, such as Camembert and Neufchâtel, which are staples of the region's cuisine. For a more authentic experience, try some fresh Normandy cider or freshly baked pastries from the local bakeries.

4. Isigny-sur-Mer and its Dairy Delights:
If you're in Isigny-sur-Mer, a visit to its local market is a must for fans of dairy products. Known for its butter and cream, the market offers some of the best Norman dairy products in the region. You can also pick up fresh seafood from the nearby Isigny Bay and browse the colorful stalls filled with fruits, vegetables, and local handmade crafts.

5. Local Farmers' Markets in the Countryside:
For a truly authentic experience, visit one of Normandy's smaller farmers' markets in towns like Beuvron-en-Auge or Bayeux, where you'll find fresh, locally grown produce and homemade goods. These markets provide a wonderful opportunity to

interact with local farmers and artisans, all while picking up unique products that reflect the true flavors of the region.

Dining for Every Budget

Normandy offers an impressive range of dining options that cater to all tastes and budgets. Whether you're looking for a casual bite at a local café or a gourmet experience at a Michelin-starred restaurantThere's something for everyone in the region.

1. Street Food and Casual Dining:
Normandy's street food scene is perfect for those on the go, offering delicious local dishes served in a casual, affordable setting. Head to the bustling streets of Rouen or Honfleur, where you can sample classic French sandwiches like the croque-monsieur or indulge in crêpes filled with Norman cheese, ham, or chocolate. The galettes, or savory buckwheat crêpes, are a must-try, especially when filled with fresh, local ingredients like eggs, cheese, and mushrooms.

2. Bistro Dining:
For a cozy and more traditional dining experience, Normandy is home to numerous bistros where you

can enjoy authentic, rustic dishes at affordable prices. Many of these bistros focus on Norman specialties, offering dishes like coq au cidre (chicken cooked with cider), duck breast, and boudin noir (blood sausage). Cafés in towns like Caen and Deauville are perfect for a relaxed meal with a glass of Normandy cider or a refreshing Kir Normand (a cocktail made with apple cider and blackcurrant liqueur).

3. Fine Dining:
For those seeking an upscale dining experience, Normandy is home to a number of Michelin-starred and gourmet restaurants. In cities like Deauville and Honfleur, you'll find sophisticated eateries where the cuisine is inspired by the sea and local produce. Seafood lovers can enjoy lobster, scallops, and fish dishes that reflect the freshest catches from the English Channel.

One standout fine dining destination is Le Pré des Lavandières, a Michelin-starred restaurant in Deauville that focuses on seasonal and locally sourced ingredients. For a more traditional fine dining experience, visit Le Caprice, also in Deauville, which offers classic French cuisine with a Norman twist.

4. The Perfect Picnic:
For a more casual but equally satisfying experience, why not enjoy a picnic in one of Normandy's beautiful outdoor settings? Visit a local market to pick up fresh bread, cheese, and charcuterie, and find a spot by the beach, in a village square, or by the Seine River. Normandy's beautiful countryside and coastal views provide the perfect backdrop for a relaxed, gourmet picnic.

Cooking Classes and Food Tours

For food lovers who want to dive deeper into Normandy's culinary traditions, cooking classes and food tours offer the perfect opportunity to learn the art of Norman cuisine from local chefs and experts.

1. Cooking Classes:
Several cooking schools and local chefs in Normandy offer hands-on cooking classes that teach you how to prepare traditional dishes using local ingredients. In Caen, you can take part in a Normandy Cooking Class, where you'll learn to make Camembert-based dishes, fish stews, and apple-based desserts. These classes often focus on

traditional farm-to-table cooking, and many chefs will even take you to the local markets to select ingredients.

In Bayeux, you can learn to prepare a classic Norman apple tart and pair it with freshly made Calvados. These cooking experiences are a great way to take home a piece of Normandy's culinary culture and recreate the flavors of the region in your own kitchen.

2. Food Tours:

For those who prefer to explore Normandy's gastronomy through guided experiences, food tours are an excellent way to immerse yourself in the region's flavors. In Honfleur, food tours offer tastings of fresh seafood, cheese, and local ciders, while exploring the charming streets of this artistic town. Rouen also has food tours that showcase the city's medieval influence on the local cuisine, with tastings of pâté, duck, and Norman desserts.

These tours often include visits to local markets, artisan workshops, and cheese producers, where you can learn firsthand about the production process and taste the freshest ingredients the region has to offer.

3. Wine and Cider Tasting Tours:
For those interested in the world of Normandy's beverages, wine and cider tours are a fantastic way to discover the nuances of Calvados and local ciders. Many tours are led by experts who explain the distilling process and the history of cider making in the region. Some tours also include tasting sessions, where you can sample a variety of ciders, Calvados, and Norman wines, learning about the different flavors and production techniques.

Normandy's cuisine is an experience in itself—rich in history, culture, and flavor. From the fresh seafood on the coast to the apple-based drinks and hearty dishes of the countryside, the region offers a truly diverse and unforgettable culinary journey. Whether you're enjoying a picnic in the fields, exploring local markets, or indulging in gourmet dining, Normandy's food scene will surely leave you wanting more.

Chapter 8: Outdoor Adventures in Normandy

Hiking the Normandy Coastal Path

Normandy's coastline offers some of the most dramatic and scenic views in all of France, making it a perfect destination for hiking enthusiasts. The Normandy Coastal Path, or GR223, spans over 400 kilometers along the region's cliffs, beaches, and charming seaside villages. Whether you're an experienced hiker or a beginner, this trail provides various sections suited to all levels of fitness, offering stunning views and breathtaking landscapes at every turn.

1. The D-Day Beaches and Beyond:
The Normandy Coastal Path is not only a journey through nature but also through history. One of the most significant stretches of the trail runs along the D-Day beaches, where hikers can visit the Omaha Beach Memorial, Juno Beach, and the Normandy American Cemetery. These historical sites are an important part of the GR223, and hiking here provides a reflective and moving experience.

The path itself meanders along the cliffs of Utah Beach, where breathtaking views of the English Channel stretch out before you. The landscape is diverse, shifting from sandy beaches to rocky headlands, and the changing scenery is perfect for photographers looking to capture Normandy's natural beauty.

2. The Cliffs of Étretat:
Further along the coastal path, the Étretat cliffs offer one of the most iconic views of Normandy. The dramatic white chalk cliffs, including the famous Arch and Needle, have inspired artists and writers for generations. The hike along this stretch of the trail rewards visitors with spectacular panoramas, and you can explore the Étretat Gardens, which offer a unique blend of art, nature, and culture. The path here is relatively easy, making it accessible to casual hikers while still providing incredible views of the Norman coastline.

3. The Cotentin Peninsula:
As you make your way westward, the Cotentin Peninsula provides a more remote and rugged experience. This stretch of the Normandy Coastal Path is marked by windswept dunes, secluded beaches, and marshlands, creating a peaceful environment far removed from the bustling tourist

hotspots. The Sainte-Mère-Église area is also rich in history, offering the chance to explore Normandy's World War II landmarks as you hike through the countryside.

4. Practical Information:

- **Best Time to Hike:** The best months for hiking along the Normandy Coastal Path are spring and fall, when the weather is mild, and the trails are less crowded. Summer can be busy, especially around popular towns like Honfleur and Étretat, so consider visiting in the shoulder seasons for a more tranquil experience.
- **Trail Difficulty:** The GR223 is a moderate to easy trail suitable for all levels of hikers. However, some sections of the trail along the cliffs can be steep and challenging, so it's important to wear sturdy shoes and carry plenty of water.

Cycling Through the Pays d'Auge

For those who prefer exploring Normandy on two wheels, cycling through the Pays d'Auge is an exceptional way to experience the region's countryside. Known for its rolling hills, apple orchards, and quaint villages, the Pays d'Auge offers quiet roads, scenic routes, and a peaceful atmosphere that's perfect for cycling enthusiasts of all levels. Whether you're looking for a leisurely ride or a more challenging route, Normandy's cycling paths provide endless opportunities for exploration.

1. The Scenic Route Through Apple Orchards:
The Pays d'Auge is famous for its apple production, and cycling through this area allows you to see the apple orchards in full bloom during the spring and summer months. The gentle hills and quiet country lanes make for a relaxing ride, where you'll pass traditional farmhouses, half-timbered cottages, and fields of flowers. Many cyclists choose to start their journey in Lisieux, a charming town that serves as a great base for exploring the Pays d'Auge.

The Route des Cidres (Cider Route) is one of the most popular cycling routes in this area. This circular route takes you through some of the region's best cider-producing villages, where you can stop at local cider farms to taste Normandy's famous ciders and Calvados. Along the way, you'll also pass through forests, meadows, and small villages, each with its own charm and history.

2. A Tour of the Norman Villages:
Cycling through the Pays d'Auge also provides the opportunity to visit some of Normandy's most picturesque villages, such as Beuvron-en-Auge, Cambremer, and Pont-l'Évêque. These towns are full of Norman charm, with their medieval architecture, flower-lined streets, and historic churches. Cycling here allows you to explore at your own pace, stopping to admire the architecture, sample local produce, and soak in the atmosphere of these peaceful rural villages.

3. Challenging Routes and Stunning Views:
For experienced cyclists looking for a more challenging route, the Pays d'Auge's rolling hills provide some excellent climbs and long descents. The Route des Abbayes, which takes you through several historical abbeys in the region, offers a slightly more difficult route, with steeper inclines and longer distances. Along the way, cyclists are rewarded with panoramic views of the lush countryside, perfect for taking in the beauty of Normandy from a higher vantage point.

4. Practical Information:

- **Best Time to Cycle:** The spring and early autumn months are ideal for cycling in

Normandy, as the weather is mild, and the countryside is lush and vibrant. Summer can be warm, but it's also the peak tourist season, so expect busier roads and more cyclists on the paths.
- **Cycling Tours:** Several guided cycling tours are available in the Pays d'Auge, offering a chance to explore the region with an expert guide who can provide insight into the local history, culture, and cider-making traditions. These tours often include stops at local farms and historic sites, making for an educational and enjoyable experience.

Sailing and Watersports on the Manche

The **Manche** region, which borders the **English Channel**, offers one of the best locations in France for **sailing** and **watersports**. With its **rugged coastline**, **tranquil coves**, and **strong winds**, the area is a favorite for those looking to explore the waters of Normandy, whether for leisurely sailing or thrilling activities like windsurfing and kite surfing.

- **1. Sailing Adventures:**
 The coastline of the **Manche** is dotted with picturesque harbors, making it an ideal destination for **sailing** enthusiasts. Towns

such as **Granville**, **Cherbourg**, and **Saint-Vaast-la-Hougue** are well-equipped with **marinas**, offering boat rentals and sailing tours. Whether you're an experienced sailor or a novice, you can take part in **guided sailing excursions** that explore Normandy's **dramatic cliffs**, hidden **beaches**, and the **scenic coastline**. These boat trips often include visits to **nearby islands**, such as **Chausey Islands**, offering a unique perspective of the region from the water.

- **2. Windsurfing and Kite Surfing:**
 For those looking for an adrenaline rush, **windsurfing** and **kite surfing** are incredibly popular on the **Manche** coast, particularly around the **Granville** and **Barfleur** areas. The **consistent winds** and **open waters** make it a **perfect spot** for both beginners and more advanced riders. Numerous schools along the coast offer equipment rentals and lessons for those new to the sport. With the water gently lapping the shoreline, these activities provide a great way to explore the coastline while having fun.
- **3. Kayaking and Paddleboarding:**
 For a more relaxed yet equally rewarding

experience, kayaking and **stand-up paddleboarding (SUP)** are popular choices for exploring the coastline and nearby rivers. Paddleboard rentals can be found in towns like **Honfleur** and **Deauville**, where you can glide over the calm waters of the **Seine River** or venture out into the English Channel. Kayaking through the **calm estuaries** or along secluded beaches provides a peaceful and intimate way to experience the stunning natural surroundings.

4. Practical Information:

- **Best Time for Watersports:** The summer months, from **June to September**, are ideal for water-based activities, with warmer temperatures and generally calm seas. However, for **sailing** and **windsurfing**, the spring and fall months also offer good conditions with **consistent winds** and fewer crowds.

- **Accessibility:** Several **watersport schools** along the coast offer **rentals** and **guiding services** for beginners and experienced enthusiasts alike. Whether you're interested in a leisurely sailing experience or a more adventurous watersport, there's something for everyone.

Exploring the Natural Reserves

Normandy is not just about its **coastline** and **historical landmarks**—it's also a **nature lover's paradise**, with an array of **protected natural reserves** that offer a peaceful escape into the wild beauty of the region. From **wetlands** to **forests** and **wildlife-rich marshlands**, these natural reserves provide a chance to experience Normandy's **breathtaking landscapes** and abundant wildlife.

1. The Cotentin and Bessin Marshes Regional Natural Park:

The **Cotentin and Bessin Marshes** is one of Normandy's most famous **natural parks**, offering an incredible variety of landscapes. Covering **over 100,000 hectares**, this park is a **biodiversity hotspot**, home to numerous **wetland species** and rare **wildlife**. Visitors can explore the marshes on **foot**, **by bike**, or **on a boat**, with guided tours available to learn more about the ecology of the region. The **park's lagoons**, **canals**, and **salt flats** are ideal for birdwatching, as it is home to many migratory species, including **herons**, **ducks**, and **waders**.

2. The Normandy Regional Nature Park:

Located in the **Pays de la Loire** region, the **Normandy Regional Nature Park** stretches from the **Seine River** to the **Pays de Bray**, offering a diverse range of **natural habitats**. This park is a haven for hikers, with over **600 kilometers** of trails winding through **forests**, **hills**, and **villages**. The park is also home to a rich variety of **wildlife**, including **foxes**, **deer**, and **boar**, as well as a **wide range of birds**. The landscape is dominated by the lush **Norman countryside**, dotted with traditional **stone farmhouses** and **apple orchards**.

3. The Marais du Cotentin Nature Reserve:

For those looking to immerse themselves in one of Normandy's most beautiful natural habitats, the **Marais du Cotentin** is a **must-visit**. This vast **wetland** reserve offers an oasis of **peace and tranquility**, with winding **canals** and **wildflower meadows**. It is an important site for **bird migration**, making it ideal for **birdwatching**. The area is home to several species of **wading birds**, **waterfowl**, and **wildlife**, making it perfect for nature lovers.

4. The Forest of Écouves:

If you're seeking a **forest adventure**, the **Forest of Écouves** offers a stunning escape into nature.

Located in the **Orne department**, this large forest is ideal for those who enjoy hiking, cycling, and **wildlife watching**. The **forest's varied terrain** includes **wooded paths**, **rivers**, and **rolling hills**, making it perfect for outdoor exploration. In the spring and summer, visitors can enjoy the **vibrant colors** of the **wildflowers** and the sounds of **birdsong**.

5. Practical Information:

- **Best Time to Visit:** The **spring** and **autumn months** are ideal for exploring Normandy's **natural reserves**, as the weather is mild, and the landscapes are at their most vibrant. Spring brings **wildflowers**, while autumn offers **changing leaf colors** that make the parks even more beautiful.

- **Activities:** Most of the reserves offer opportunities for **hiking**, **birdwatching**, **cycling**, and **boating**. Be sure to check local visitor centers for information on guided tours and nature walks.

Normandy's Beaches

Normandy is home to some of the most beautiful and diverse **beaches** in France, from the **wide sandy shores** of the **Côte Fleurie** to the **rugged cliffs** of the **Côte d'Albâtre**. Whether you're looking for a relaxing day by the sea or an active **water sport adventure**, Normandy's beaches have something for everyone.

1. The Beaches of Deauville and Trouville-sur-Mer:

The **beaches of Deauville** and **Trouville-sur-Mer** are the epitome of **French coastal elegance**. With their **golden sands** and **iconic beach huts**, these beaches offer the perfect setting for a **leisurely day** in the sun. The area is popular for beachgoers who prefer a more **sophisticated experience**, with plenty of **seafront cafés**, **boutiques**, and **restaurants** to enjoy. Both towns also offer **water sports** such as **surfing**, **windsurfing**, and **kite surfing**, making them ideal for active beachgoers.

2. The Wild Beaches of Cotentin:

For those seeking a more **wild** and **secluded experience**, the **beaches of Cotentin** provide a beautiful, untouched landscape. The **sand dunes** and **wide beaches** of **Barfleur, Utah Beach**, and **Sainte-Mère-Église** offer a quiet space to relax and enjoy the natural beauty of the **Normandy coast**. These beaches are perfect for **swimming**, **beachcombing**, and simply unwinding in **peaceful surroundings**.

3. The Cliffs and Beaches of Etretat:

The **cliffs of Etretat** are famous for their **dramatic views** and **breathtaking landscapes**, but the beaches at the foot of the cliffs are equally beautiful. The **pebbled shores** offer a perfect spot to **sunbathe**, swim, or relax, while the surrounding cliffs provide an iconic backdrop for any beach outing. **Rock climbing** is also a popular activity in the area, offering an exciting way to explore the coastline.

4. Watersports and Activities:

Normandy's beaches also offer an array of **water sports** for adventure seekers. Whether you want to try your hand at **windsurfing**, **kite surfing**, **jet skiing**, or **stand-up paddleboarding**, the region provides plenty of opportunities to get in the water. The **Côte de Nacre** is particularly popular for **windsurfing**, thanks to its **consistent winds**. **Kayaking** and **sailing** are also popular on the region's calmer beaches, such as those near **Honfleur** and **Deauville**.

5. Practical Information:

- **Best Time to Visit: Summer** is the best time to enjoy Normandy's beaches, with **warm temperatures** and long days perfect for swimming and beach activities. However, the shoulder months of **spring** and **autumn** offer quieter beaches and a more relaxed atmosphere.

- **Facilities:** Many of Normandy's more popular beaches, like those in **Deauville** and **Trouville**, are equipped with **lifeguards**, **restaurants**, and **changing facilities**, making them perfect for a day by the sea with all the comforts.

Whether you're drawn to the **Manche's windswept waters** for sailing and windsurfing, the **natural reserves** for hiking and wildlife watching, or the region's **beautiful beaches** for relaxation and watersports, **Normandy** offers a wealth of **outdoor adventures** for every traveler. Its stunning landscapes, from **cliffs** to **rolling hills**, provide the perfect backdrop for outdoor activities, making it an ideal destination for those who seek both adventure and serenity in nature.

MAP OF ÉTRETAT

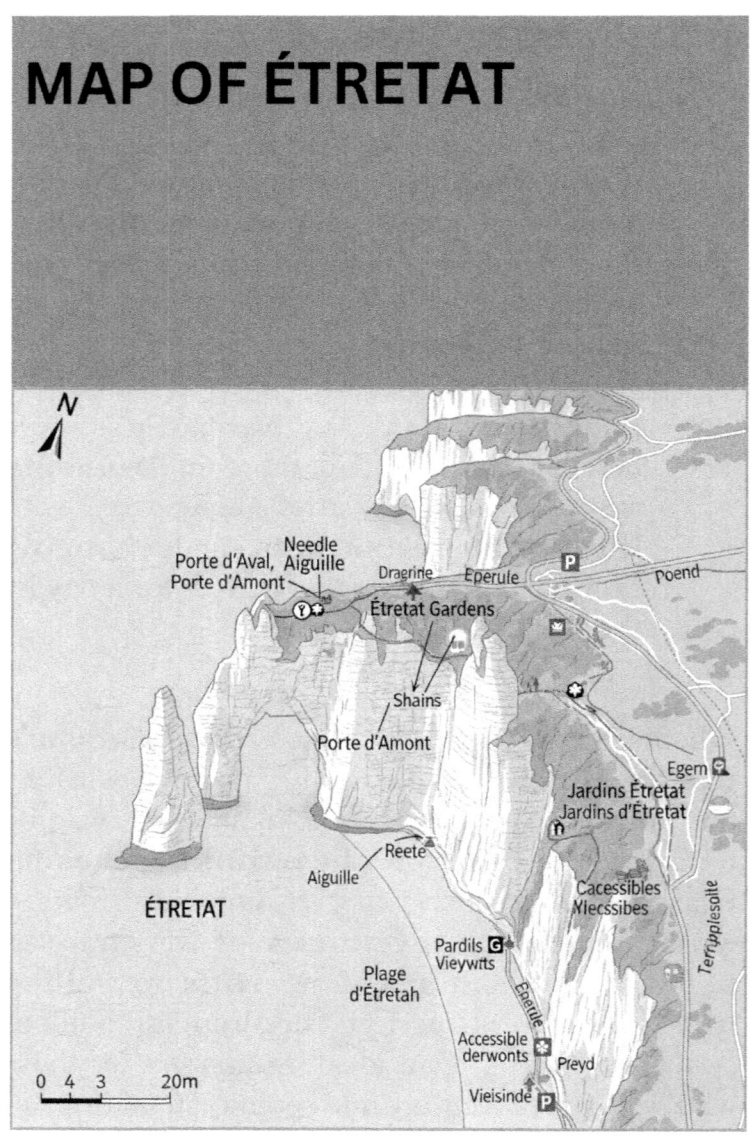

Chapter 9: Family-Friendly Normandy

Best Activities for Children

Normandy is a region that is both rich in history and natural beauty, making it an excellent destination for families. From interactive museums to historic sites and outdoor adventures, Normandy offers a range of activities that will both entertain and educate children of all ages.

1. The Cité de la Mer (Cherbourg):
For families with young children, the Cité de la Mer in Cherbourg is an engaging and educational experience. This maritime museum is dedicated to the history of the sea, and it offers a variety of exhibits that are interactive and fun for children. The Aquarium is home to an impressive array of sea creatures, and the submarine experience allows kids to step inside a real submarine for a fascinating tour of its inner workings. The museum's interactive displays ensure that children are not only entertained but also gain insight into maritime history and marine life.

2. The Abbaye de Jumièges (Jumièges):

The Abbaye de Jumièges, one of the most famous Norman abbeys, is a wonderful family-friendly destination. The ruins of the abbey are surrounded by gardens and lush grounds, which make for a great space for kids to run and explore. The site is both educational and fun for children, as it offers an introduction to medieval architecture and Norman history. There are also family activities available throughout the year, such as guided tours and workshops on medieval life.

3. The Museum of the Battle of Normandy (Bayeux):

While Bayeux is known for its famous tapestry, the Museum of the Battle of Normandy provides an engaging and interactive way for families to learn about World War II. The museum uses life-size exhibits, photographs, and multimedia to help explain the historical significance of the D-Day landings and the Battle of Normandy. The exhibits are designed to be informative yet accessible, and there are special family tours that make the history more relatable for children.

4. Zoological Park of Cerza (Hermival-les-Vaux):
For animal lovers, the Zoological Park of Cerza, located near Lisieux, is a wonderful family attraction. This safari park allows families to get up close with wild animals from around the world. With over 1,000 animals, including lions, giraffes, and elephants, children will love exploring the park and learning about the different species. There are also play areas, interactive exhibits, and educational talks that make the experience fun and educational.

5. The Normandy Tank Museum (Catz):
For families with children who are interested in military history or machines, the Normandy Tank Museum in Catz is a unique experience. The museum showcases a collection of tanks, military vehicles, and artifacts from World War II. There are also live demonstrations and interactive exhibits that provide a fun way for children to learn about history while engaging with the exhibits.

6. D-Day Landing Beaches (Various Locations):
Visiting the D-Day landing beaches can be an educational experience for older children, offering them an opportunity to learn about the historical significance of World War II. Sites like Omaha

Beach, Utah Beach, and Juno Beach have family-friendly visitor centers and interactive exhibits that provide a younger audience with an understanding of the events that took place on June 6, 1944. These sites offer an important lesson in history while providing a beautiful setting for a family day out.

Outdoor Adventures for the Family

Normandy's diverse landscapes make it an ideal place for outdoor adventures that the whole family can enjoy. Whether you're hiking through forests, cycling through countryside, or exploring the beaches, Normandy offers countless outdoor activities perfect for families.

1. Hiking in the Suisse Normande:
The Suisse Normande is a region of Normandy known for its rolling hills, rugged cliffs, and lush greenery. The area offers family-friendly hikes that are not too strenuous, making them ideal for children to enjoy. The Orne River runs through the region, providing stunning views and plenty of opportunities for a peaceful family walk or picnic by the river. The trails offer a mix of wooded paths, meadows, and vistas, perfect for kids to explore while learning about the region's natural beauty.

2. Cycling through the Pays d'Auge:

Cycling through the picturesque Pays d'Auge is a wonderful way for families to experience Normandy's apple orchards, rolling hills, and charming villages. The area's network of quiet, flat roads makes it perfect for family bike rides. You can cycle past half-timbered cottages, traditional farmhouses, and beautiful landscapes, stopping along the way to sample local cider or visit farms producing Camembert. Many rental shops offer family bikes and child seats, making it an easy and fun activity for all ages.

3. Kayaking on the River Orne:

For a more adventurous outdoor activity, try kayaking or canoeing along the Orne River. The calm waters and scenic surroundings make it an ideal activity for families with children. Many rental companies offer kayak rentals, along with guided tours of the river and its picturesque surroundings. Children will enjoy paddling through the natural reserves and spotting wildlife, while parents can enjoy the peacefulness of the water and the stunning Norman countryside.

4. Exploring the Beaches:

Normandy's beaches are perfect for families, offering a mix of water sports, relaxation, and nature exploration. Whether you visit the golden sands of Deauville and Trouville-sur-Mer or the more rugged shores of Utah Beach and Juno Beach, families will find plenty of activities to enjoy. Kids can build sandcastles, swim, and explore the tide pools, while parents can relax and take in the breathtaking coastal views. Many beaches also offer water sports rentals, such as stand-up paddleboarding, windsurfing, and kite surfing, making them ideal for families who want to try something more active.

5. Adventure Parks and Playgrounds:
For families with younger children, there are several adventure parks and playgrounds around Normandy. Parks like La Récré des 3 Curés near Carentan offer a fun mix of rides, games, and play areas that are perfect for kids of all ages. Parc Zoologique Cerza and Parc du Bocasse also offer interactive experiences, animal encounters, and playgrounds that ensure a fun day for families with young children.

Kid-Friendly Museums and Interactive Experiences

Normandy offers a range of **interactive museums** and **hands-on experiences** that are perfect for engaging children while learning about the region's **history**, **culture**, and **natural wonders**. These museums provide fun and **educational activities** that capture the imagination of young visitors, ensuring that both kids and adults have an unforgettable experience.

1. The Musée de la Tapisserie de Bayeux (Bayeux Tapestry Museum):

- The **Bayeux Tapestry Museum** in the town of **Bayeux** is a must-see for families. While the **Bayeux Tapestry** itself is a fascinating historical artifact, the museum also offers interactive displays that explain the story behind the tapestry in a child-friendly manner. Children can use **interactive screens** and **digital guides** to better understand the **Norman Conquest of England** in 1066. The museum also has a **kids' area**, where younger visitors can explore **miniature versions** of the tapestry and learn about medieval life.

2. The Cité de la Mer (Cherbourg):

- As mentioned earlier, the **Cité de la Mer** is a perfect family destination. This **maritime museum** in **Cherbourg** offers a series of interactive exhibits about **marine biology**, **submarines**, and **the history of sea exploration**. Children can step aboard a real **submarine**, explore the **Aquarium**, and enjoy a variety of hands-on activities, such as **touch tanks** with sea creatures and interactive displays about the **deep sea**. It's both fun and educational for kids of all ages.

3. The Musée des Automates (Lisieux):

- For kids fascinated by **mechanical toys** and **automata**, the **Musée des Automates** in **Lisieux** offers a unique experience. This museum showcases a vast collection of **automaton dolls**, **miniature moving figures**, and **historical models**. The museum's interactive displays allow children to interact with **moving exhibits** and learn about the evolution of mechanical toys, from early wind-up models to modern robotic creations.

4. The Le Musée de la Vie Maritime (Honfleur):

- This family-friendly museum, located in the historic port town of **Honfleur**, provides an interactive exploration of **Normandy's maritime history**. The museum features hands-on exhibits, **model ships**, and the opportunity for children to try out **nautical navigation games** and puzzles. It also offers workshops and educational programs for families to enjoy together.

5. The Parc Zoologique de Clères (Clères Zoo):

- The **Clères Zoo** is a **kid-friendly animal park** located near **Rouen**. The zoo offers a **natural environment** for various species of **wildlife** and **exotic animals**, including **baboons**, **wolves**, **big cats**, and a variety of **birds**. The park's **interactive educational programs** and **animal feeding demonstrations** make it a great place for children to engage with nature. There are also **play areas** and **paved walking paths**, making it easy for families with younger children to enjoy a leisurely day out.

Exploring Normandy's Gardens and Parks

Normandy is not only rich in history but also boasts a stunning variety of **gardens** and **parks**, perfect for families who want to explore the beauty of nature. These green spaces offer both **peaceful retreats** and **interactive activities** that will delight children and adults alike.

1. Monet's Garden in Giverny:

- One of the most famous gardens in the world, **Claude Monet's garden in Giverny** is a must-visit for families. The **water garden** with its iconic **Japanese bridge** and **water lilies** is perfect for children to explore while learning about the connection between art and nature. The **flower garden** is equally enchanting, bursting with colors in **spring** and **summer**. Families can enjoy a **guided tour** of the gardens and **art workshops** designed to teach children how to create their own nature-inspired artwork, making it both fun and educational.

2. The Jardin des Plantes (Rouen):

- The **Jardin des Plantes** in **Rouen** is a large, public garden perfect for a family day out. With over 20,000 plant species, a **botanical garden**, and a **zoological section** housing various species of animals, the park offers something for every member of the family. **Children's workshops** and educational programs are available, teaching kids about the **importance of biodiversity** and the natural world.

3. The Château de Vendeuvre Gardens:

- Located in the **Pays d'Auge** region, the **gardens of Château de Vendeuvre** are a delight for families. The **manicured gardens**, with their **ornate fountains**, **flower beds**, and **shaded walks**, provide a peaceful setting for a family stroll. Kids will love exploring the **labyrinth garden** and seeing the **miniature vegetable garden** that is designed to teach about organic farming. The castle also has a small **museum** of miniature furniture, adding a cultural element to the visit.

4. Parc de la Vallée (Caen):

Parc de la Valée in **Caen** is a great family-friendly park with expansive **lawn areas**, **wooded sections**, and **playgrounds** for children. This park offers plenty of space for picnics, games, and relaxation while enjoying views of the **river** and **nature reserves**. The park is also home to seasonal events and festivals that children will enjoy, including **outdoor concerts** and **themed festivals**.

5. The Forêt d'Écouves (Ecouves Forest):

For families who love adventure, **Ecouves Forest** near **Alençon** is a wonderful place to explore. This forest offers **hiking trails**, **wildlife spotting**, and **nature walks**, making it ideal for children to engage with nature. With educational programs about the **flora and fauna** of the region, this is a great destination for families looking to get outdoors and learn together.

Normandy with Kids

When traveling with children, finding the right **accommodation** and **family-friendly dining** options is key to ensuring a comfortable and enjoyable experience. Normandy offers a range of **family-friendly hotels**, **gîtes**, and **restaurants** that cater to both children and adults.

1. **Family-Friendly Accommodations:**

- **Gîtes** (holiday cottages) in Normandy are perfect for families, offering **spacious** accommodations, **self-catering options**, and access to **private gardens** or **outdoor spaces**. Many gîtes are located in **quaint villages** or near **natural parks**, making them ideal for a relaxed family getaway.

- **Château Hotels**: For families looking for a more **luxurious experience**, several **château hotels** in Normandy offer family suites, children's activities, and access to **beautiful grounds** for exploration. These hotels provide a unique opportunity to stay in a **historic castle** while enjoying the comforts of modern amenities.

- **Farm Stays**: For a more hands-on experience, consider staying at one of Normandy's **working farms**, where children can interact with animals, learn about farming practices, and explore the countryside.

2. Family Dining in Normandy:

- Normandy is known for its **gourmet food**, but there are also plenty of **family-friendly restaurants** that offer **kid-friendly menus**, **interactive dining experiences**, and **local specialties** that both adults and children will love. Look for **crêperies** and **bistros**, where kids can enjoy classic dishes like **crêpes**, **French fries**, and **Norman apple desserts**.
- **Crêperies** are a favorite with kids, offering sweet or savory crêpes that are easy for young children to enjoy. Many crêperies in **Bayeux** and **Deauville** have a **play corner** or **children's menu**, allowing for a relaxing meal with the family.

- **Norman Bistros** often have hearty **family meals** like **duck**, **pork**, and **seafood** dishes. Many restaurants also offer **special menus for children**, including simpler, smaller portions of local dishes like **mussels** and **fish**, making it easier for families to dine together.

3. Farm-to-Table Dining:

- Normandy's focus on **local produce** and **seasonal ingredients** makes it easy to find healthy, fresh options for children. Many restaurants offer **farm-to-table** dining, where children can try **fresh vegetables**, **local cheeses**, and **Norman meats**, often sourced from nearby farms.

Chapter 10: Shopping and Souvenirs

Local Crafts and Artisan Goods

Normandy's rich history, cultural heritage, and traditional craftsmanship make it a fantastic place for picking up unique souvenirs. From handmade goods to local specialties, the region offers a wide array of artisan products that reflect the artistry and traditions of Normandy. Whether you're seeking something for yourself or a gift for a loved one, Normandy's local crafts and artisan goods make the perfect keepsakes to bring home.

1. Camembert and Local Cheeses:
Camembert cheese, the pride of Normandy, is one of the best gifts you can bring home. While it's available throughout France, buying it directly from a local farm or cheese shop adds an extra layer of authenticity. You can also pick up other Norman cheeses, such as Livarot, Pont-l'Évêque, and Neufchâtel, which are equally delicious and offer a wider variety of flavors. Many of the cheese dairies offer packaging designed for travel, so you can bring these cheese varieties home with ease.

2. Norman Cider and Calvados:

Normandy is renowned for its cider and Calvados (apple brandy), both of which make excellent gifts and souvenirs. The region's apple orchards are celebrated for producing high-quality apples that are transformed into award-winning ciders and the region's signature Calvados. Many local cider houses offer bottled varieties of these drinks for sale, as well as gift sets that include both cider and Calvados. Visit a local distillery or cider farm for a guided tasting, where you can purchase your favorite bottles to take home.

3. Norman Pottery:

Normandy is home to some of France's most well-known pottery traditions, especially in the Coutances and Villedieu-les-Poêles areas. Handmade ceramics and earthenware are common souvenirs, often painted with bright floral patterns or scenes of rural life. Traditional Norman pots, bowls, and plates make a wonderful addition to any kitchen, as they capture the essence of Norman craftsmanship. Look for shops or workshops where you can purchase hand-painted pottery directly from the artisan.

4. Lace and Embroidery:
Normandy lace and embroidery are renowned for their intricate designs and historical significance. Honfleur and Caen are two great places to find shops specializing in lace and hand-stitched textiles. These beautifully crafted pieces, such as lace napkins, embroidered tablecloths, and decorative pillows, make for elegant and timeless gifts. Many artisans also offer personalized or custom-made embroidered items, perfect for a special keepsake.

5. Norman Wooden Toys and Craftwork:
For something a little different, Norman wooden toys are a great souvenir, especially for families with children. These hand-carved toys reflect the woodworking tradition of Normandy and are often made using local woods. Look for traditional wooden boats, miniature farm animals, and puzzles that have been carefully crafted by local artisans. These items not only serve as beautiful keepsakes but also offer a glimpse into the region's craftsmanship and traditions.

6. Norman Textiles and Fashion:
In addition to the traditional crafts, Normandy is also known for fashion and textiles. If you're looking for something stylish, pick up a striped

sailor shirt (known as marinière), a staple in Norman fashion. These shirts are typically made from cotton and feature the iconic navy and white stripes, representing the maritime heritage of the region. You can find marinières at local boutiques, along with other handmade accessories, such as scarves, hats, and leather bags, crafted by local artisans.

Normandy's Antiques

Normandy's antique shops and flea markets are treasure troves for those looking to find unique, historical pieces from the region's rich past. The area is home to ancient buildings, family estates, and charming villages where old treasures are handed down through generations. Whether you're a collector of vintage items or simply searching for a memorable and one-of-a-kind piece to bring home, Normandy's antique stores are full of surprises.

1. Antique Markets and Brocantes:
One of the best ways to explore Normandy's antique scene is by visiting the brocantes (flea markets) held throughout the region. These markets often feature a mix of vintage furniture, antique jewelry, porcelain, and household items dating back to the 18th and 19th centuries. The flea markets in Rouen,

Honfleur, and Caen are particularly well-known, offering everything from rustic French farm tools to charming old paintings and collectible ceramics.

2. Norman Furniture and Decor:
Normandy has a long tradition of woodworking and furniture making, and you'll find beautiful antique furniture at many of the region's specialist shops. Look for Norman-style armoires, chests, and side tables, often crafted from oak and featuring hand-carved detailing. These pieces reflect the elegant yet functional style that has defined the region's interior design for centuries.

3. Vintage Art and Collectibles:
For art lovers, Normandy's antique galleries are full of vintage artwork and framed prints that showcase the region's history and landscapes. You might come across watercolors of Normandy's beaches, etchings of medieval towns, or oil paintings from the Impressionist movement that began in Honfleur. Many antique shops also carry vintage postcards, maps, and photographs, providing a glimpse into the past for collectors.

4. Normandy's Maritime Antiques:
Given the region's strong maritime heritage, you'll also find a selection of maritime antiques in

Normandy. From vintage ship models to old maritime charts and nautical instruments, these items offer a direct connection to the sea-faring past of Normandy. Shops near the Côte de Nacre or Le Havre are especially known for their sea-themed antiques, offering unique finds for those interested in maritime history.

5. Practical Tips for Antique Shopping:

- **Know What You're Looking For:** Normandy is home to a wealth of antique treasures, so it's best to have an idea of the type of items you're interested in (e.g., furniture, jewelry, or artwork). This will help you navigate the various markets and shops more effectively.
- **Bargaining:** While most antique shops have set prices, flea markets and brocantes are often more flexible, and haggling is encouraged. Don't hesitate to negotiate if you feel comfortable doing so.
- **Shipping:** If you purchase larger items, such as furniture, ask about shipping options. Many stores can arrange delivery of your purchases to your home.

The Best Shops in Honfleur, Deauville, and Bayeux

Normandy's vibrant towns and cities are full of charming boutiques, artisan shops, and local markets that offer visitors a chance to take home unique pieces from the region. Whether you're looking for handcrafted goods, designer fashion, or local produce, Normandy's key shopping destinations—Honfleur, Deauville, and Bayeux—are home to a range of wonderful shops that cater to all tastes and budgets.

1. Honfleur: Charming Shops and Art Galleries

The picturesque town of Honfleur is not only famous for its historic port and artistic legacy but also for its delightful shopping scene. Stroll through its narrow streets, where you'll find a mix of boutiques, art galleries, and local artisan shops.

- **Art Galleries and Paintings:** Honfleur has long been a favorite among artists, particularly the Impressionists, so it's no surprise that the town is home to a variety of art galleries. You can purchase original paintings, prints, and photographs that capture the stunning landscapes of

Normandy. The Galerie du Vieux Honfleur and Galerie Art et Emotions are two of the best spots to find local artwork.

- **Handcrafted Goods and Pottery:** The Côte de Grâce area of Honfleur is known for its handcrafted pottery and artisan goods. Many of the local shops offer handmade ceramics, including vases, plates, and bowls featuring vibrant Norman designs.

- **Fashion and Accessories:** Honfleur is also home to several boutiques offering unique fashion and accessories. Shops like Les Jardins de Sophie and L'Atelier d'Emma specialize in French-chic clothing, leather handbags, and stylish jewelry. These shops offer timeless, high-quality pieces that reflect the town's sophisticated atmosphere.

2. Deauville: Luxury and Designer Shopping
Deauville is known for its glamorous atmosphere, and its shopping scene matches the town's chic reputation. With its high-end boutiques and luxury fashion shops, Deauville offers a wide variety of exclusive items that are perfect for those looking to indulge in a bit of retail therapy.

- **Designer Fashion:** Deauville is home to several high-end fashion stores offering the latest designs from both French and international brands. You can find shops like Chanel, Louis Vuitton, and Hermès for luxury clothing, accessories, and leather goods. For fashion lovers, Deauville's Rue Victor Hugo is a must-visit shopping street.

- **Beauty and Skincare Products:** If you're looking for luxurious beauty products, Deauville offers several specialized beauty shops and spas that feature premium skincare lines, including French cosmetic brands like Dior and Guerlain. These are perfect for picking up gifts or pampering yourself with the finest French beauty.

- **Jewelry and Accessories:** For a touch of elegance, visit Deauville's jewelry boutiques where you can find high-quality silver and gold pieces, watches, and vintage jewelry. The Galerie du Casino and Bijouterie Mathilde offer an array of fine pieces for those looking for something special.

3. Bayeux: History and Heritage Shopping

The historic town of Bayeux is not only famous for its Bayeux Tapestry but also for its selection of traditional shops and local crafts. Whether you're searching for historical memorabilia or handmade products, Bayeux offers a variety of unique finds.

- **Bayeux Tapestry Souvenirs:** A trip to Bayeux wouldn't be complete without purchasing a souvenir inspired by the famous Bayeux Tapestry. Many shops around the Bayeux Tapestry Museum offer replica tapestries, printed fabrics, postcards, and historical books about the Norman Conquest, making them a perfect gift for history buffs.

- **Handmade Pottery and Ceramics:** Bayeux is home to several ceramic shops offering Norman-style pottery, from colorful plates to vases and bowls. Many of the shops also offer custom designs that reflect the Norman countryside, perfect for a personalized gift.

- **Antique and Vintage Finds:** Bayeux also boasts a number of antique shops, where you can find unique vintage pieces, from furniture and militaria to jewelry and artifacts. Les Antiquités du Drapeau is one of the best places to hunt for hidden treasures that showcase the region's rich history.

Exploring Normandy's Flea Markets

For those who love to hunt for hidden gems and enjoy the thrill of a flea market, Normandy offers several brocantes (flea markets) where you can find everything from vintage clothing to antiques and collectibles.

1. Rouen Flea Market:
Rouen, one of Normandy's largest cities, hosts a lively flea market that takes place on select weekends throughout the year. The market offers a wide selection of secondhand goods, vintage furniture, antique porcelain, and collectible items. It's the perfect place to search for unique souvenirs or find something special for your home.

2. Honfleur Flea Market:
Honfleur's flea market is held in the Place Saint-Catherine and is a great spot for those looking for local antiques, vintage textiles, and crafts. The market also features local handmade items, such as

wooden toys and Norman pottery, making it a wonderful place to find unique, high-quality gifts.

3. Caen Flea Market:
The flea market in Caen is a popular destination for antique lovers. Held in the Place Saint-Pierre, the market features a wide variety of items, including old books, vintage furniture, artworks, and military memorabilia. It's a treasure trove for collectors and anyone looking for authentic Norman antiques.

4. Deauville's Sunday Market:
Deauville's Sunday market is a lively and vibrant experience, with fresh produce, local cheeses, and artisan goods for sale. While not a traditional flea market, it offers a wonderful selection of local handicrafts and souvenirs, including jewelry, handmade scarves, and local wines.

A Shopper's Guide to Normandy

Normandy is home to a wealth of unique gifts and souvenirs that capture the essence of the region's artistic, historical, and natural heritage. Whether you're shopping in the luxury boutiques of Deauville, the charming shops of Honfleur, or the historical streets of Bayeux, there's no shortage of options for those looking to take home a piece of Normandy's charm.

- **Norman Cheese and Cider:** A visit to Normandy isn't complete without sampling or bringing home local cheeses like Camembert and Livarot. Pair them with a bottle of Norman cider or Calvados for the perfect gourmet gift.
- **Norman Pottery and Ceramics:** From handmade pottery to vintage ceramics, Normandy's artisan crafts are among the region's most cherished souvenirs. Look for Norman plates, bowls, and vases in towns like Honfleur and Bayeux.
- **Antiques and Collectibles:** For history buffs and collectors, Normandy's antique shops and flea markets offer an array of unique finds, from militaria to vintage furniture and Norman art.
- **Local Fashion and Accessories:** Don't miss the local boutiques in Deauville and Honfleur, where you can find French-chic fashion, designer handbags, and stylish jewelry that reflect the region's elegance.

From the charming artisan goods of Honfleur to the luxurious fashion of Deauville and the historical treasures of Bayeux, Normandy offers a diverse and rewarding shopping experience. Whether you're seeking unique local crafts, vintage finds, or luxury fashion, the region's markets, shops, and galleries provide plenty of opportunities to take home a piece of Normandy's culture and craftsmanship.

Chapter 11: Normandy After Dark

A Taste of Normandy's Nightlife

When the sun sets over Normandy, the region comes alive with a vibrant nightlife scene that blends traditional French charm with a modern twist. Whether you're looking for a quiet evening at a café overlooking the seaside, an elegant dinner in a historic town. Normandy offers a variety of options to suit all tastes. The region's nightlife embraces the relaxed pace of life in Normandy, with plenty of places to unwind after a day of sightseeing.

1. Fine Dining Restaurants:
For a special night out, Normandy is home to numerous fine dining restaurants that offer a taste of gourmet French cuisine. Deauville and Trouville-sur-Mer boast several Michelin-starred restaurants, such as Le Ciro's, known for its exquisite seafood and elegant atmosphere, or La Belle Époque, offering a blend of traditional and innovative Norman dishes in an upscale setting. These restaurants provide the perfect ambiance for a romantic dinner or a celebratory evening.

2. Late-Night Options:
While Normandy is generally more relaxed compared to cities like Paris, there are still several spots for those who enjoy a lively late-night scene. Rouen has a growing number of nightclubs and music venues, where you can enjoy electronic music or live bands until the early hours. In Deauville, the Le Bar du Casino offers a mix of cocktails, dancing, and occasional live music performances, while Cabaret Normandy hosts burlesque shows and performances in a more glamorous setting.

Theatrical Performances and Music Festivals

Normandy's cultural scene thrives after dark, with a rich array of theatrical performances and music festivals that celebrate the region's artistic talent. Whether you're into classical music, jazz, or contemporary theatre, there's no shortage of performances to enjoy during the evening hours.

1. Theatres and Live Performances:
For theater lovers, Normandy offers an array of theatre productions that range from classic French plays to contemporary performances. The Comédie-Française in Rouen is one of the region's top venues, hosting a mix of classical French plays and more modern, experimental shows. For a more

intimate experience, check out Le Théâtre de Caen, which often stages both classical and contemporary works.

2. Normandy's Music Scene:
From classical concerts to jazz festivals, Normandy is home to a vibrant music scene that caters to a variety of tastes. The Normandy Chamber Orchestra and Rouen Opera House host performances throughout the year, showcasing both local and international musicians. If you prefer something a little more upbeat, Deauville and Honfleur offer live jazz clubs and swing bands that create an energetic atmosphere.

3. Music Festivals:
Normandy is known for its celebration of music and the arts, with a variety of music festivals taking place throughout the year. One of the biggest events is the Normandy Impressionist Festival, which celebrates the region's connection to the Impressionist movement through a series of music concerts, art exhibitions, and performances that showcase the region's cultural history.
In Deauville, the Jazz à Deauville festival attracts world-renowned jazz musicians, filling the town's streets and concert halls with lively performances each year. The Festival of Saint-Romain in Rouen is

another well-known event, offering an impressive lineup of classical music performances held in stunning historical venues.

4. Outdoor Concerts and Festivals:
In the warmer months, Normandy offers outdoor music festivals that take advantage of the region's stunning natural settings. The Festival Normandie Impressionniste features open-air performances, and concerts are held at various historic venues, including castles, gardens, and beaches. The Les Plages Musicales in Trouville-sur-Mer offers free concerts on the beach, creating a relaxed environment where visitors can enjoy music while watching the sunset.

Nighttime Strolls and Historical Tours

Normandy's history and natural beauty don't fade when the sun sets. As the day winds down, the region's historical landmarks, medieval streets, and seaside towns take on a new charm, making them perfect for nighttime strolls and historical tours. Exploring Normandy after dark allows visitors to experience its rich past in a completely different light—literally and figuratively.

1. Strolling Through Honfleur's Harbor at Night:
One of Normandy's most picturesque towns, Honfleur takes on an even more magical atmosphere as evening descends. The charming old harbor, lined with colorful wooden houses and art galleries, is beautifully illuminated at night, making it an ideal location for a romantic stroll. As you walk along the quay, you can admire the reflections of the buildings in the water and soak in the peaceful ambiance. Cafés and restaurants lining the harbor offer cozy spots to stop for a drink and take in the sights.

For a deeper dive into Honfleur's history, consider joining a night walking tour. These guided tours take visitors through the medieval streets, offering fascinating insights into the town's fishing heritage, artistic legacy, and the role it played during World War II. As dusk settles, Honfleur's quaint streets and charming architecture create a uniquely atmospheric experience.

2. Rouen's Illuminated Historic Center:
Rouen, the capital of Normandy, is known for its stunning Gothic architecture and rich history. At night, the medieval town center comes to life, especially around the Place du Vieux-Marché and Rouen Cathedral. The cathedral's façade, which

inspired several paintings by Claude Monet, is lit up at night, creating a striking scene against the dark sky.

You can also take part in historical walking tours of Rouen by night, which reveal the city's fascinating past, from its medieval roots to its role during the French Revolution and Joan of Arc's trial. The tours bring Rouen's ancient streets to life, offering a unique perspective on the town's history, with stories of royalty, religion, and rebellion.

3. Bayeux's Historic Strolls:

Bayeux, home to the famous Bayeux Tapestry, is a charming town that feels even more captivating after sunset. The medieval streets and half-timbered houses are beautifully lit, and you can take a leisurely evening walk along the Aure River. The reflection of the Bayeux Cathedral in the water is one of the most picturesque sights in the region.

In addition to its visual appeal, Bayeux's night tours provide an opportunity to learn more about the town's history, including its connection to William the Conqueror and the Norman Conquest of England. With fewer crowds and the charm of the evening light, this is the perfect way to explore Bayeux at a more relaxed pace.

4. Mont Saint-Michel After Dark:
For those seeking a truly unique experience, Mont Saint-Michel at night is a must-see. As the crowds thin out and the island fortress becomes illuminated, you'll feel as if you've stepped back in time. The medieval streets, abbey, and church take on a mystical quality as you walk around the island's cobblestone paths. Many visitors choose to experience Mont Saint-Michel through a nighttime guided tour, which provides a magical atmosphere for exploring its ancient ramparts, monastic halls, and chapels. The towering abbey at the top of the island is even more impressive when lit up against the night sky.

Chapter 12: Suggested Itineraries

3 Days: Normandy's Highlights in a Nutshell

If you're short on time but still want to experience the best of Normandy, this 3-day itinerary offers a perfect overview of the region's most iconic sights, rich history, and breathtaking landscapes. This condensed version of Normandy's highlights is ideal for travelers who want to get a taste of the region without feeling rushed.

Day 1: Historical Normandy and D-Day Landmarks

- **Morning:** Start your journey with a visit to the Bayeux Tapestry Museum in Bayeux. This world-famous tapestry is an unmissable piece of history, and the museum offers a fascinating insight into the Norman Conquest of England.

- **Lunch:** Enjoy a meal at one of Bayeux's local bistros, where you can sample traditional Norman dishes like duck confit or Norman apple tart.

- **Afternoon:** Head towards the D-Day beaches, with stops at Omaha Beach, Utah Beach, and the Normandy American Cemetery. These landmarks provide a sobering and poignant look at World War II history and Normandy's role in the D-Day invasion.

- **Evening:** Spend the evening in Honfleur, a beautiful harbor town known for its artistic history and stunning waterfront views. Stroll along the quayside, browse local art galleries, and enjoy dinner at a harbor-side restaurant.

Day 2: Seaside Charm and Norman Heritage

- **Morning:** Visit Mont Saint-Michel, one of France's most iconic landmarks. Explore the medieval abbey perched on the island and enjoy panoramic views of the surrounding coastline.

- **Lunch:** Enjoy a leisurely seafood lunch at one of the local eateries on the island, offering fresh seafood and regional specialties.

- **Afternoon:** After Mont Saint-Michel, head towards the Côte Fleurie, visiting Deauville and Trouville-sur-Mer. These elegant seaside resorts offer stunning beaches, luxury shopping, and beautiful promenades. Take a walk along the boardwalk or visit the Deauville Casino for a taste of the local nightlife.

- **Evening:** Dine in Deauville at one of the charming bistros offering a mix of local seafood, Norman cheeses, and regional wines.

Day 3: Normandy's Countryside and Culinary Delights

- **Morning:** Explore the Pays d'Auge region, famous for its apple orchards and charming villages. Start with a visit to the Abbey of Saint-Wandrille, a peaceful retreat set amid the countryside, before heading to the apple farms for a tour and tasting session of local cider and Calvados.

- **Lunch:** Stop for lunch in one of the picturesque villages like Beuvron-en-Auge, enjoying Norman dishes such as Camembert cheese paired with fresh bread and cider.

- **Afternoon:** Visit Honfleur's charming shops and galleries before heading to the Château de Caen, a medieval fortress that showcases Normandy's rich history. Explore the castle, which also houses the Musée de Normandie and the Musée des Beaux-Arts.

- **Evening:** End your trip with a relaxed dinner in Caen, where you can sample more local specialties, including Norman cider and pâté de foie gras.

7 Days: A Deep Dive into Normandy's Culture and Coastline

For travelers who want to immerse themselves in Normandy's culture, history, and natural beauty, a 7-day itinerary provides a more in-depth experience, offering a chance to explore beyond the region's major attractions and discover its hidden gems.

Day 1: Arrival and Introduction to Bayeux

- **Morning:** Arrive in Bayeux, home of the famous Bayeux Tapestry. Start your trip with a visit to the Bayeux Tapestry Museum to view this incredible historical artifact.

- **Lunch:** Enjoy lunch in the historic center of Bayeux, sampling local specialties such as duck and Norman apple tart.

- **Afternoon:** Explore the town of Bayeux, including its gothic cathedral and charming medieval streets.

- **Evening:** Dine at one of Bayeux's local bistros or restaurants, savoring dishes prepared with fresh, local ingredients.

Day 2: The D-Day Beaches and Normandy's WWII Legacy

- **Morning:** Head to the D-Day beaches, including Omaha Beach, Utah Beach, and the Normandy American Cemetery. These significant historical sites provide an emotional and educational experience of the events of June 6, 1944.

- **Lunch:** Enjoy a simple yet satisfying meal in Arromanches, a town that played a key role in the D-Day landings.

- **Afternoon:** Visit the Juno Beach Centre to explore Canada's role in the D-Day landings and the Pegasus Bridge Museum, where you can learn about the strategic importance of the bridge during the Normandy invasion.

- **Evening:** Spend the evening in Honfleur, strolling along its harbor and enjoying a relaxed dinner in one of its many waterfront restaurants.

Day 3: Mont Saint-Michel and the Normandy Coast

- **Morning:** Visit Mont Saint-Michel for a full day exploring this stunning abbey and medieval village perched on the island.

- **Lunch:** Enjoy lunch on the island, savoring local seafood dishes like moules marinières (mussels in white wine sauce).

- **Afternoon:** Explore the island's shops and cafes before wandering the cobblestone streets and soaking in the atmosphere.

Evening: Return to Saint-Malo or Avranches for dinner at a seaside restaurant.

Day 4: The Countryside and Normandy's Cider Route

- **Morning:** Head to the Pays d'Auge for a day dedicated to Normandy's cider and apple heritage. Visit local cider farms for a tour and tasting of Calvados and Norman cider.

- **Lunch:** Enjoy a traditional Norman lunch at a local farmhouse or cider house, paired with Camembert cheese and fresh bread.

- **Afternoon:** Explore the beautiful village of Beuvron-en-Auge, one of the most beautiful villages in France, before heading to Pont-l'Évêque for more tastings of local cheeses and ciders.

- **Evening:** Return to Lisieux or Caen for a relaxed dinner, enjoying more Norman specialties.

Day 5: The Beaches of Deauville and Trouville-sur-Mer

- **Morning:** Spend the morning in Deauville, one of Normandy's most famous seaside resorts. Visit Deauville Beach and take a walk along the boardwalk, enjoying views of the English Channel.

- **Lunch:** Have lunch at a seaside café, enjoying fresh seafood and Norman cider.

- **Afternoon:** Head to Trouville-sur-Mer, a charming neighboring seaside town. Stroll through the fishing port and visit the local fish market to see the freshest catches.

- **Evening:** Enjoy dinner in Trouville at one of its many traditional restaurants, specializing in Normandy's seafood.

Day 6: Rouen's History and Culture

- **Morning:** Spend the day in Rouen, Normandy's historic capital. Visit the Rouen Cathedral, known for its Gothic architecture and its connection to Claude Monet.

- **Lunch:** Enjoy a casual lunch in one of Rouen's quaint cafés or bistros, sampling local dishes like Norman apple chicken or cassoulet.

- **Afternoon:** Explore the Vieux-Marché, the Joan of Arc Memorial, and Rouen's medieval quarter, full of half-timbered houses and charming streets.

- **Evening:** Attend a performance at the Rouen Opera House or enjoy a wine tasting in one of the city's wine bars.

Day 7: Final Day in Honfleur and the Normandy Coast

- **Morning:** Spend the final day in Honfleur, exploring the charming port town known for its vibrant art scene. Visit the Eugène Boudin Museum to view works inspired by the town's landscapes.

- **Lunch:** Enjoy a leisurely lunch at a harbor-side restaurant, indulging in more Norman seafood or a classic French pastry.

- **Afternoon:** Take a final stroll through Honfleur's quaint streets, visiting art galleries, local shops, and enjoying the picturesque views of the harbor.

- **Evening:** Celebrate your last night in Normandy with a delicious dinner at a Michelin-starred restaurant or local bistro, savoring the region's finest dishes.

10 Days: A Perfect Blend of History, Countryside, and Seaside Relaxation

For those who have more time to truly immerse themselves in Normandy's diverse landscapes, rich history, and charming towns, this 10-day itinerary provides the ultimate blend of culture, countryside, and seaside relaxation. This itinerary offers a leisurely pace, allowing you to explore the region's iconic landmarks, enjoy its natural beauty, and experience its laid-back coastal charm, all while immersing yourself in its medieval heritage.

Day 1: Arrival in Rouen – Normandy's Historic Heart

- **Morning:** Arrive in Rouen, Normandy's historic capital. Begin your trip with a visit to the Rouen Cathedral, famous for its Gothic architecture and its connection to Claude Monet. Explore the Vieux-Marché, where Joan of Arc was martyred.

- **Lunch:** Enjoy lunch in Place du Vieux-Marché, sampling classic Norman dishes like duck confit or a hearty bowl of cassoulet.

- **Afternoon:** Wander through Rouen's medieval streets, admiring the half-timbered houses and the Norman art on display at the Musée des Beaux-Arts. If time allows, take a boat ride along the Seine River for views of the town from the water.

- **Evening:** Dinner at a traditional bistro in Rouen, offering a selection of local wines and ciders.

Day 2: D-Day Landmarks – A Journey Through History

- **Morning:** Head to the D-Day beaches, starting with Omaha Beach and Utah Beach, both pivotal sites in the Normandy Invasion of 1944. Visit the Normandy American

Cemetery for a moving tribute to those who fought here.

- **Lunch:** Stop for lunch at a seaside café in Arromanches, where you can sample seafood dishes like mussels and fish stew.

- **Afternoon:** Explore the Juno Beach Centre (Canada's contribution to D-Day) and visit Pegasus Bridge, a site of strategic importance during the landings. These attractions offer important insights into Normandy's role in World War II.

- **Evening:** Stay overnight in Honfleur, enjoying its peaceful atmosphere and waterfront dining options.

Day 3: Honfleur and Deauville – Artistic Heritage and Seaside Elegance

- **Morning:** Explore Honfleur's charming harbor, art galleries, and wooden houses. Visit the Eugène Boudin Museum for a glimpse into the town's artistic heritage.

- **Lunch:** Have a leisurely lunch at a harbor-side restaurant, enjoying fresh seafood and a glass of Normandy cider.

- **Afternoon:** Continue your journey to Deauville, a town known for its luxurious resorts and elegant boutiques. Take a walk along the boardwalk and enjoy the beach views.

- **Evening:** Dinner at Deauville's high-end restaurant, serving local specialties paired with Norman wines.

Day 4: Mont Saint-Michel – Normandy's Iconic Landmark

- **Morning:** Visit Mont Saint-Michel, one of France's most iconic landmarks. Spend the day exploring the abbey and the medieval streets that wind their way up to the island's summit. Learn about its history and architectural significance.

- **Lunch:** Have lunch on the island, choosing from a selection of local specialties like mussels, Norman cider, and apple-based desserts.

- **Afternoon:** Continue exploring the abbey and surrounding fortifications before enjoying a peaceful walk along the island's causeway.

- **Evening:** Stay overnight in Saint-Malo, a historic seaside city known for its fortifications and breathtaking coastal views.

Day 5: Saint-Malo and the Pink Granite Coast

- **Morning:** Explore the cobblestone streets of Saint-Malo and visit the walled city for a sense of its maritime history. Climb to the city walls for panoramic views of the coastline and English Channel.

- **Lunch:** Enjoy a seafood lunch at one of the harbor-side restaurants, offering fresh fish, oysters, and shellfish.

- **Afternoon:** Drive along the Pink Granite Coast to Plouha and Perros-Guirec, known for their striking coastal landscapes and dramatic rock formations. Explore the coastal paths and relax on the beautiful beaches.

- **Evening:** Overnight in Saint-Malo, enjoying a leisurely dinner at a local bistro serving local seafood and traditional dishes.

Day 6: The Pays d'Auge – Cider, Cheese, and Charming Villages

- **Morning:** Head inland to the Pays d'Auge region, famous for its apple orchards and local cheeses. Stop by Lisieux, a town known for its Basilica of Sainte-Thérèse and its historical connection to Norman cider.

- **Lunch:** Visit a local cider house for a tour and tasting, sampling Calvados and Norman cider. Enjoy a traditional Norman lunch paired with cheese and freshly baked bread.

- **Afternoon:** Explore the picturesque villages of Beuvron-en-Auge and Cambremer, both famous for their Norman charm and traditional architecture.

- **Evening:** Spend the evening in Caen, exploring its historical center and enjoying dinner at one of the local bistros offering traditional Norman specialties.

Day 7: The Beaches of Deauville and Trouville-sur-Mer

- **Morning:** Head to Deauville for a day of seaside relaxation. Stroll along the beach, visit the Deauville casino, or browse the elegant boutiques and fashion shops.

- **Lunch:** Enjoy lunch at a seaside café in Trouville-sur-Mer, a neighboring beach town with a charming port and traditional French charm.

- **Afternoon:** Take a boat trip along the Seine estuary or visit the villages along the coast. Spend the rest of the day relaxing on the beach or visiting local museums.

- **Evening:** Enjoy dinner at a local restaurant serving French cuisine with a view of the beach and seaside promenade.

Day 8: The Cotentin Peninsula – Coastal Beauty and Nature Reserves

- **Morning:** Travel to the Cotentin Peninsula to explore the wild beaches, salt marshes, and bird reserves of the region. Start with a visit to Carentan, a town known for its WWII history and nature reserves.

- **Lunch:** Stop at a local restaurant serving seafood, and enjoy views of the coastline.

- **Afternoon:** Visit the Bessin Regional Natural Park and explore the wetlands by kayak or on foot. You'll have the chance to spot wildlife and enjoy scenic views of the Norman countryside.

- **Evening:** Return to Saint-Vaast-la-Hougue, a seaside town known for its seafood restaurants and historic fortifications.

Day 9: The Normandy Countryside – A Day of Peace and Relaxation

- **Morning:** Visit the tranquil abbeys and châteaux scattered throughout Normandy's countryside. Château de Caen offers a look into the region's medieval history, while the Abbey of Saint-Wandrille provides a peaceful retreat for reflection.

- **Lunch:** Enjoy lunch at a local vineyard or farmhouse, sampling fresh, organic produce and locally made cheeses.

- **Afternoon:** Spend the afternoon exploring the Seine Valley, where the region's lush greenery and tranquil rivers provide a relaxing atmosphere for a gentle walk or bike ride.

- **Evening:** End your day with a relaxing dinner at a countryside bistro, where you can enjoy Norman meats and cheese, followed by a glass of Calvados.

Day 10: Final Day in Honfleur and Relaxation

- **Morning:** Spend your last day in Honfleur, exploring the charming harbor and its art galleries. Take a stroll through the old town, and enjoy the beautiful harbor views.

- **Lunch:** Enjoy lunch at one of the waterfront cafés, sampling local seafood or Norman specialties.

- **Afternoon:** Spend your final afternoon shopping in Honfleur boutiques, and enjoy the peaceful atmosphere before your departure.

The Ultimate Normandy Road Trip

For those seeking the freedom to explore Normandy at their own pace, there's no better way to experience the region's breathtaking coastlines, quaint villages, and historical landmarks than by embarking on a road trip. This 7-day itinerary is designed to guide you through the best of Normandy—from its Norman beaches to its medieval towns, apple orchards, and charming countryside—with plenty of time to relax and enjoy the journey.

Day 1: Rouen – Normandy's Historic Heart

- **Morning:** Start your road trip in Rouen, Normandy's historic capital. After arriving, head straight for the Rouen Cathedral, one of the finest examples of Gothic architecture in France. Don't miss the Joan of Arc Memorial and the Vieux-Marché (Old Market Square), where Joan of Arc was executed.

- **Lunch:** Enjoy lunch in the Vieux-Marché district at one of the local bistros, where you can try dishes like duck confit or Norman cheeses.

- **Afternoon:** After lunch, take a stroll through the medieval streets of Rouen, with its half-timbered houses and art galleries. For history enthusiasts, a visit to the Musée des Beaux-Arts is a must, showcasing a variety of Norman art.

- **Evening:** Head to Honfleur for an overnight stay, and enjoy dinner at a harbor-side restaurant, where you can savor seafood and local cider.

Day 2: Honfleur and Deauville – Seaside Charm

- **Morning:** Start your day by exploring Honfleur, a beautiful harbor town with a rich artistic history. Visit the Eugène Boudin Museum and take a walk around the charming Place Sainte-Catherine.

- **Lunch:** Enjoy a relaxed lunch at one of Honfleur's seaside cafés, sampling fresh seafood or Norman specialties.

- **Afternoon:** Drive to Deauville, known for its glamorous atmosphere and stunning beach. Walk along the boardwalk, visit the Deauville casino, and admire the luxury shops that line the streets.

- **Evening:** Spend the night in Deauville, enjoying dinner at one of the town's high-end restaurants or local bistros, offering exquisite seafood dishes and Calvados.

Day 3: Mont Saint-Michel – The Island Abbey

- **Morning:** Depart Deauville and make your way to Mont Saint-Michel, one of the most iconic landmarks in France. Spend the day exploring the abbey, the medieval streets, and the island's fortifications.

- **Lunch:** Enjoy a traditional seafood lunch on the island, with dishes like mussels and fish stew paired with local cider.

- **Afternoon:** Continue exploring Mont Saint-Michel, and be sure to visit the abbey's stunning cloisters and the historical museums that highlight the island's past.

- **Evening:** Drive to Saint-Malo for a stay in this historic seaside city. Take a stroll along the walled city and enjoy a dinner overlooking the coastline.

Day 4: Saint-Malo and the Pink Granite Coast

- **Morning:** Explore Saint-Malo in the morning, visiting the Fort National, Saint-Malo Cathedral, and the walled city. You can also visit the twin fortresses of Saint-Vaast-la-Hougue before continuing your journey along the Pink Granite Coast.

- **Lunch:** Stop for lunch at one of the local seafood restaurants in Saint-Malo or along the coastline, and sample some of the freshest fish and shellfish available.

- **Afternoon:** Head towards Plouha and Perros-Guirec, two of the most scenic spots on the Pink Granite Coast. Walk along the coastal paths and marvel at the unique rock formations and stunning views.

- **Evening:** Stay in Plouha or Perros-Guirec for the night, enjoying a relaxed dinner in a local restaurant offering Normandy specialties.

Day 5: The Cotentin Peninsula – A Peaceful Escape

- **Morning:** Head towards the Cotentin Peninsula, where you can enjoy a more peaceful, off-the-beaten-path experience. Begin your day with a visit to Carentan and its WWII sites.

- **Lunch:** Stop in the charming village of Barfleur, one of the most beautiful in Normandy. Enjoy lunch at a local bistro overlooking the port and sea, with a focus on Norman seafood.

- **Afternoon:** Explore the Bessin Regional Natural Park, famous for its wetlands and wildlife, offering a chance to connect with nature.

- **Evening:** Spend the night in Saint-Vaast-la-Hougue, a historic town known for its fortifications and delicious seafood restaurants.

Day 6: The Pays d'Auge – Cider, Cheese, and Countryside Charm

- **Morning:** Leave the Cotentin Peninsula and head towards the Pays d'Auge region, which is famous for its apple orchards and cheese production. Visit a local cider farm for a tasting session and learn about the region's cider-making traditions.

- **Lunch:** Enjoy a traditional lunch at a local farmhouse, where you can sample Camembert cheese, freshly baked bread, and Norman cider.

- **Afternoon:** Drive through the beautiful villages of Beuvron-en-Auge and Cambremer, stopping for photo opportunities along the way. Visit Pont-l'Évêque, the town known for its cheese.

- **Evening:** Overnight in Caen, where you can enjoy dinner at a local bistro offering a mix of Norman specialties and regional wines.

Day 7: Normandy's Beaches and Return to Rouen

- **Morning:** Spend the morning on Normandy's beaches, such as those in Trouville-sur-Mer or Deauville, where you can enjoy a relaxing walk along the coast or participate in water activities like surfing or windsurfing.

- **Lunch:** Stop for lunch at a seaside café, where you can enjoy a fresh seafood platter with a glass of local cider.

- **Afternoon:** Take the scenic route back to Rouen, making stops at the Abbaye de Jumièges and the Château de Caen.

- **Evening:** End your road trip with a final dinner in Rouen, enjoying a delicious meal that showcases the best of Normandy's cuisine.

Normandy with Kids: A Family-Friendly Adventure

Normandy is a fantastic destination for families, offering a mix of outdoor adventures, cultural experiences, and educational activities that appeal to both children and adults. This 3-day family-friendly itinerary is designed to give you a balanced experience of Normandy's history, seaside charm, and nature while keeping kids entertained along the way.

Day 1: Arrival in Rouen – Exploring the Historic City

- **Morning:** Arrive in Rouen, where children can enjoy a fun, interactive visit to the Rouen Cathedral and the Joan of Arc Memorial.

- **Lunch:** Have a family lunch at one of Rouen's casual cafés, offering kid-friendly options such as pâté and salads.

- **Afternoon:** Visit the Musée des Beaux-Arts, where children can explore the exhibits with child-friendly guides or take part in workshops.

- **Evening:** Explore the medieval streets of Rouen at a relaxed pace, and have dinner at a family-friendly restaurant.

Day 2: Deauville and Trouville-sur-Mer – A Seaside Day

- **Morning:** Head to Deauville, where kids can play on the beach, build sandcastles, or ride bikes along the coastal path.

- **Lunch:** Enjoy lunch at a beachside café, where kids can try French pastries and simple seafood dishes.

- **Afternoon:** Explore Trouville-sur-Mer, a neighboring beach town that offers children's playgrounds and small art galleries.

- **Evening:** Stay in Deauville, where you can dine in a relaxed setting that caters to families.

Day 3: Mont Saint-Michel – The Abbey on the Island

- **Morning:** Visit Mont Saint-Michel for a family-friendly adventure. The kids will love exploring the narrow streets, visiting the abbey, and learning about its history.

- **Lunch:** Enjoy a picnic near the island or dine at a local restaurant offering family-sized portions.

- **Afternoon:** Continue exploring the island and take a family-friendly guided tour to learn about its medieval architecture and history.

- **Evening:** Head to Saint-Malo for dinner and overnight accommodation.

This 3-day itinerary offers families the chance to explore the best of Normandy—from historical sites and natural beauty to seaside fun and family-friendly activities. The region offers plenty of opportunities for kids to learn, play, and relax, making it an ideal destination for family vacations.

Chapter 13: Practical Travel Information

Essential French Phrases for Travelers

While English is widely spoken in tourist areas across Normandy, knowing a few key French phrases can greatly enhance your experience and help you connect with locals. The people of Normandy are known for their hospitality, and making an effort to speak their language will be appreciated. Here are some essential French phrases for travelers:

1. Greetings and Basic Phrases:

- Bonjour (bohn-zhoor) – Good morning / Hello
- Bonsoir (bohn-swahr) – Good evening
- Merci (mehr-see) – Thank you
- S'il vous plaît (seel voo pleh) – Please
- Excusez-moi (ex-kew-zay mwah) – Excuse me
- Oui (wee) – Yes
- Non (noh) – No

- Comment ça va ? (koh-mohn sah vah) – How's it going?
- Ça va bien, merci. (sah vah byan mehr-see) – I'm fine, thank you.

2. Directions and Travel:

- Où est... ? (oo eh) – Where is...?
- Comment puis-je aller à... ? (koh-mohn pwee-zh ah-lay ah) – How can I get to...?
- Je suis perdu(e) (zhuh swee pehr-doo) – I'm lost (add "e" for females)
- Aidez-moi, s'il vous plaît ! (ay-day mwah seel voo pleh) – Help me, please!
- La gare (lah gahr) – Train station
- L'arrêt de bus (lah-ray duh booss) – Bus stop
- Combien ça coûte ? (kohm-byen sah koot) – How much does it cost?

3. Dining and Shopping:

- L'addition, s'il vous plaît. (lah-dee-syon seel voo pleh) – The bill, please.
- Un café, s'il vous plaît. (uh kah-fay seel voo pleh) – A coffee, please.
- Avez-vous... ? (ah-vay voo) – Do you have...?
- Je voudrais... (zhuh voo-dray) – I would like...

- C'est délicieux ! (seh day-lee-syu) – It's delicious!

4. Emergencies:

- Appelez un médecin ! (ah-peh-lay uh meh-deh-seen) – Call a doctor!
- J'ai perdu mon passeport. (zhay pehr-doo mon pah-spoh) – I've lost my passport.
- Où est l'hôpital ? (oo eh loh-pee-tal) – Where is the hospital?

These basic phrases will help you navigate through most interactions, from ordering food at a café to asking for directions. Locals will appreciate your efforts, even if you don't speak perfectly!

Travel Insurance, Currency Exchange, and Connectivity

1. Travel Insurance:
Travel insurance is highly recommended for anyone visiting Normandy, as it can help cover unexpected issues like medical emergencies, cancellations, and lost luggage. Some key benefits of travel insurance include:

- **Medical coverage:** In case you need medical attention during your trip, including hospital stays or emergency medical evacuation.
- **Trip cancellations:** If you have to cancel or cut your trip short due to unforeseen circumstances, travel insurance can help you recover lost costs.
- **Lost or delayed baggage:** Compensation for lost luggage or delayed baggage can help ease the inconvenience.
- **Flight delays and interruptions:** Insurance can provide compensation for any expenses incurred due to flight delays or cancellations.

Ensure your policy covers activities you plan to do in Normandy, such as hiking, water sports, or driving a rental car.

2. Currency Exchange:
Normandy, like the rest of France, uses the Euro (€) as its currency. While credit cards are widely accepted in most cities and towns, it's a good idea to have some cash on hand, especially when visiting smaller villages or rural areas.

Currency exchange tips:

- **ATMs:** You'll find ATMs in major towns and cities like Rouen, Deauville, and Honfleur. Most ATMs accept international cards, but check with your bank to ensure your card will work in France.
- **Currency exchange offices:** These are available at major train stations and airports. While convenient, exchange rates may be less favorable, so it's best to check rates before exchanging large sums.
- **Credit cards:** Visa and MasterCard are widely accepted, but American Express may not be as commonly accepted, especially in rural areas.
- **Tips for payments:** Many French shops have a minimum amount for credit card payments (typically around €10-15). Smaller purchases may require cash.

3. Connectivity:
Staying connected while traveling is essential, whether it's for directions, online bookings, or simply keeping in touch with loved ones.

- **SIM Cards and Mobile Data:** If you're staying for an extended period, it may be worth buying a local SIM card for your phone. SFR, Orange, and Bouygues Telecom are the three main providers in France. You can buy prepaid SIM cards at local shops or at the airport. Many plans offer data bundles for tourists.

- **Wi-Fi:** Free Wi-Fi is widely available in cafes, hotels, and restaurants in larger towns and cities. Some tourist attractions also offer free Wi-Fi. You can also find Wi-Fi hotspots in many public spaces, but it's worth checking with local businesses to ensure connection.

- **Public Transportation Apps:** For ease of getting around, consider downloading apps like Citymapper, Google Maps, or SNCF (for train schedules). These apps will help you navigate the public transport system and find your way to popular attractions in Rouen, Honfleur, and other major cities.

Accessibility

Normandy is a region that welcomes travelers of all abilities, with various initiatives in place to ensure an inclusive and accessible experience for visitors with disabilities or limited mobility.

1. Accessible Attractions and Sites:

Many of Normandy's key attractions have made efforts to improve accessibility. Notable examples include:

- **Mont Saint-Michel:** The abbey is accessible via ramps and lifts, and the island itself is largely navigable for those with mobility challenges.
- **Bayeux Tapestry Museum:** The museum offers wheelchair access and is equipped with elevators to make the exhibits accessible to all visitors.
- **Rouen Cathedral:** The cathedral is accessible for visitors with limited mobility and provides wheelchair access to the main areas.

In addition to these attractions, public transportation in Rouen, Caen, and Deauville is largely wheelchair accessible, with many buses and trains offering low-floor access for easy boarding.

2. Accommodation:
Normandy offers a range of accommodations that are accessible to visitors with disabilities. Hotels, gîtes, and bed and breakfasts in major cities like Rouen and Honfleur often provide wheelchair-friendly rooms, as well as adapted bathrooms. Always check with your accommodation ahead of time to confirm specific accessibility features.

3. Beach Accessibility:
Some of Normandy's most popular beaches, including Deauville and Trouville-sur-Mer, are equipped with wheelchair access to the beach via ramps and special chairs that allow people with limited mobility to enjoy the sand and sea. Look out for handicap-accessible beaches, as these will have the necessary equipment for a safe and enjoyable experience.

4. Support Services:
For travelers requiring additional support, local tourist offices can provide useful information about accessible services, including specialized tours or transportation services. Some companies offer private guided tours designed specifically for travelers with disabilities, providing personalized services for a more comfortable experience.

Local Festivals and Events You Shouldn't Miss

Normandy is not only known for its beautiful landscapes and historical sites but also for its lively festivals and cultural events that bring the region's rich heritage to life. Whether you're visiting in the summer, fall, or spring, there's always something happening to celebrate the best of Norman culture, food, and art.

1. Normandy Impressionist Festival (Spring/Summer)

- **Location:** Throughout Normandy, with major events in Rouen, Honfleur, and Bayeux.
- **Description:** This biennial festival celebrates the Impressionist movement, with exhibitions, outdoor concerts, and performances inspired by the famous artists who once lived and worked in the region. You can visit Monet's Gardens in Giverny, see exhibitions in local museums, and enjoy open-air performances in various towns.
- **Why You Shouldn't Miss It:** Perfect for art lovers, this festival offers a chance to engage with Normandy's artistic heritage

and experience Impressionist art in the very places that inspired it.

2. The Deauville American Film Festival (September)

- **Location:** Deauville
- **Description:** Celebrating American cinema, the Deauville American Film Festival is one of the most prestigious film festivals in France. It features a series of premieres, film screenings, and awards ceremonies. Visitors can enjoy outdoor screenings, celebrity appearances, and film-related events.
- **Why You Shouldn't Miss It:** It's a glamorous event for film enthusiasts, offering a unique opportunity to see new films, meet filmmakers, and experience the buzz of an international festival in the heart of Normandy's seaside resort.

3. The Fête de la Saint-Romain (October)

- **Location:** Rouen
- **Description:** This centuries-old festival celebrates the patron saint of Rouen with a mix of historical re-enactments, medieval

games, and a traditional fair. The festival features vibrant parades, costume contests, and historical performances, bringing the city's medieval past to life.
- **Why You Shouldn't Miss It:** The festival gives visitors a chance to experience Rouen's rich history in a fun and interactive way, with costumed parades, musicians, and street performances that transport you back to the Middle Ages.

4. The Harfleur Medieval Festival (July)

- **Location:** Harfleur
- **Description:** The Harfleur Medieval Festival takes visitors on a journey through the Middle Ages, with re-enactments, jousting tournaments, and medieval crafts. The village's historic streets are transformed into a living history exhibit, with knights, craftsmen, and minstrels creating an authentic medieval atmosphere.
- **Why You Shouldn't Miss It:** It's perfect for families and history enthusiasts who want to immerse themselves in the medieval period, with plenty of interactive activities for children.

5. The Festival of Normandy (April-May)

- **Location:** Various towns across Normandy, including Caen and Rouen
- **Description:** This festival celebrates Normandy's culture, its history, and its gastronomy, with events like folk music, traditional dances, and local food tastings. Norman cider, cheese, and apple-based dishes are often highlighted during the festivities.
- **Why You Shouldn't Miss It:** It's a great way to experience local traditions and regional food, all while enjoying festivals in scenic Norman towns.

6. The Fête de la Mer (July)

- **Location:** Granville
- **Description:** The Fête de la Mer is a celebration of the sea and maritime life, featuring sailing races, fish markets, and a variety of water-based activities. There are also traditional seafood feasts and maritime parades that showcase the local fishing culture.
- **Why You Shouldn't Miss It:** For those interested in the region's maritime heritage,

this festival provides a wonderful opportunity to enjoy the coastal culture while participating in exciting activities.

Where to Get Detailed Maps

Having a detailed map is essential for navigating the stunning towns, villages, and natural landscapes of Normandy. Fortunately, there are several resources available to ensure you don't get lost and can make the most of your visit. Whether you prefer digital apps, printed maps, or tourist guides, Normandy has plenty of ways to guide your travels.

1. Google Maps and Apple Maps:

- **Available On:** Smartphones and tablets
- **Description:** These widely-used apps provide up-to-date, detailed maps for navigating both urban and rural areas in Normandy. They offer directions for driving, walking, and public transport. Google Maps also offers offline maps, which are great for when you're traveling through areas with limited data connection.

2. IGN Maps:

- **Available On:** Smartphones, tablets, and printed versions
- **Description:** The Institut Géographique National (IGN) is France's official national mapping organization, offering detailed topographic maps of Normandy. These maps are particularly useful for hiking, cycling, and exploring the rural countryside. IGN's website also provides digital maps for download.
- **Tip:** Visit IGN's online store for downloadable maps of specific regions in Normandy, including hiking and cycle routes.

3. Normandy Tourist Website:

- **Available On:** Website and app
- **Description:** The official Normandy tourism website provides a variety of interactive maps, from driving routes to specific tourist attractions. The site includes helpful maps of major cities like Rouen, Caen, and Deauville, as well as historical landmarks and natural parks. It also has downloadable PDF maps for easy offline use.

4. Komoot:

- **Available On:** Smartphones (iOS, Android)
- **Description:** For outdoor enthusiasts, Komoot is a great app for cycling and hiking in Normandy. It provides custom routes and detailed maps of trails, including Normandy's coastal path and the Pays d'Auge. This app is especially useful for those who prefer active exploration and need specific routes for outdoor adventures.

5. Local Tourist Information Centers:

- **Available In:** Major towns and tourist hubs
- **Description:** You can find printed maps and brochures at tourist information centers throughout Normandy, such as in Rouen, Deauville, Honfleur, and Caen. These centers offer free maps of local attractions, walking tours, and regional guides. They can also provide personalized advice on what to see and do based on your interests.

Local Tourist Information Centers

Normandy has a wealth of local tourist information centers that provide everything you need to make your visit smooth and enjoyable. These centers are staffed with knowledgeable locals who can offer insider tips, helpful recommendations, and maps to guide you through the region.

1. Rouen Tourist Office:

- **Location:** Place de la Cathédrale, Rouen
- **Services:** Free maps, guided tours, personalized itineraries, and tickets to local attractions like the Bayeux Tapestry Museum and Rouen Cathedral.

2. Honfleur Tourist Office:

- **Location:** 1 Place Sainte-Catherine, Honfleur
- **Services:** Detailed maps of Honfleur's harbor and art galleries, information on local festivals like the Honfleur Festival of Impressionism, and suggestions for seaside walks.

3. Deauville Tourist Office:

- **Location:** 148 Rue de la République, Deauville

- **Services:** Brochures on beach activities, shopping, and the Deauville American Film Festival. They also offer walking tours of the town and cycling maps for exploring the Normandy coastline.

4. Bayeux Tourist Office:

- **Location:** 17 Place du 6 Juin, Bayeux
- **Services:** Information on WWII sites, including the D-Day beaches, and maps of Bayeux's medieval town center. They also provide guided tours of the Bayeux Tapestry.

5. Caen Tourist Office:

- **Location:** 12 Place Saint-Pierre, Caen
- **Services:** Free walking tour maps, information on historical landmarks, and recommendations for visiting the Château de Caen and the Pegasus Bridge Museum.

These centers are a great first stop for any tourist, providing maps, guides, and helpful information that will ensure your trip is as seamless and enjoyable as possible.

From understanding the essential French phrases and securing the right travel insurance to knowing where to find detailed maps and access tourist information centers, these practical tips will help you navigate Normandy with ease. By taking advantage of these resources, you'll be well-prepared to experience the region's history, natural beauty, and culture to the fullest.

Chapter 14: Beyond Normandy

Day Trips to the Loire Valley and Mont Saint-Michel

While Normandy itself is packed with rich history, stunning landscapes, and charming villages, the region is also conveniently located for easy access to some of France's most iconic destinations. If you have a few extra days, consider taking a day trip to explore the nearby Loire Valley and Mont Saint-Michel, two extraordinary destinations that are just a short drive or train ride from Normandy.

1. Day Trip to Mont Saint-Michel: A Timeless Wonder

- **Distance from Normandy:** Approximately 1.5 to 2 hours by car

- **Why You Should Visit:** Mont Saint-Michel is one of France's most famous landmarks and a UNESCO World Heritage site. This medieval abbey, perched atop a rocky island surrounded by vast tidal flats, offers a magical experience that seems almost otherworldly.

Things to Do:

- **Explore the Abbey:** The abbey is the centerpiece of the island, offering panoramic views of the surrounding area. Visitors can explore the medieval streets, visit the church, and walk the fortifications.
- **Tidal Flats:** Time your visit with the tide change to witness the dramatic movement of the water. You can also take a guided walking tour along the tidal flats when the waters recede.
- **Island Tour:** Wander through the island's narrow streets, filled with historic houses, quaint shops, and local eateries. Stop for fresh seafood or try local pastries in one of the cafés.

Practical Tips:

- Arrive early to avoid the crowds, especially during the peak summer months.
- Consider visiting at low tide to experience the full dramatic effect of the island's surroundings.

2. Day Trip to the Loire Valley: France's Wine and Castle Region

- **Distance from Normandy:** Approximately 3 to 4 hours by car

- **Why You Should Visit:** Known as the Garden of France, the Loire Valley is famous for its vineyards, châteaux, and quaint towns. A day trip to this region offers the chance to explore grand castles, picturesque towns, and indulge in delicious local wines and produce.

Things to Do:

- **Visit Château de Chambord:** One of the most famous and stunning castles in the Loire Valley, Château de Chambord is renowned for its French Renaissance architecture and beautiful grounds. Take a guided tour through its ornate rooms, exquisite gardens, and vast estate.
- **Wine Tasting in Tours:** The town of Tours serves as a gateway to the Loire's wine region, known for its white wines, particularly Chenin Blanc. Many local wineries offer wine tours where you can taste

local wines and learn about the production process.
- **Explore Amboise:** A charming town that's home to Château d'Amboise, the royal residence of several French kings, including Francis I. Leonardo da Vinci spent his final years in Amboise, and his home is now a museum that you can visit.

Practical Tips:

- Plan ahead for the Loire Valley, as it's best known for visiting multiple castles. A guided small-group tour from Normandy is a great option for seeing the highlights without stress.
- Travel by car to give you the flexibility to visit smaller towns and vineyards that might not be accessible by public transportation.

Exploring Northern Brittany

If you're drawn to the rugged coastlines of northern France and the wild beauty of Brittany, a trip to Côtes d'Armor in Northern Brittany is an excellent way to continue your adventure beyond Normandy. This region is known for its dramatic cliffs, idyllic beaches, and quaint fishing villages—ideal for those seeking a mix of natural beauty and traditional Breton culture.

1. Day Trip to Dinan: A Medieval Gem

- **Distance from Normandy:** Approximately 1.5 to 2 hours by car

- **Why You Should Visit:** Dinan is a wonderfully preserved medieval town, offering cobbled streets, historic fortifications, and beautiful timber-framed houses. It's often considered one of Brittany's most charming towns, perfect for a leisurely stroll through time.

Things to Do:

- **Explore the Old Town:** Wander through the medieval streets, visiting landmarks like the Saint-Sauveur Basilica, the Dinan Clock Tower, and the old town walls.
- **Cruise on the Rance River:** Take a boat trip along the Rance River, which offers breathtaking views of the surrounding countryside and cliffside villages.

- **Visit the Château de Dinan:** This 14th-century castle offers stunning views over the town and the Rance River.

Practical Tips:

- Dinan is walkable, but be prepared for steep hills and narrow streets, especially around the historic center.
- Make time to visit the local cafés and enjoy a traditional Breton crepe.

2. Day Trip to Cap Fréhel and Fort La Latte: Coastal Beauty and History

- **Distance from Normandy:** Approximately 2.5 to 3 hours by car

- **Why You Should Visit:** The Cap Fréhel and Fort La Latte area offers some of Brittany's most striking coastal scenery, including high cliffs, towering lighthouses, and fortress ruins that stand above the wild Atlantic Ocean.

Things to Do:

- **Visit Cap Fréhel:** The Cap Fréhel lighthouse stands at over 70 meters tall, providing breathtaking views over the Brittany coastline. The surrounding cliffs are also home to seabirds, making this a perfect spot for nature lovers.
- **Explore Fort La Latte:** Situated atop a cliff overlooking the sea, Fort La Latte is a medieval castle dating back to the 14th century. It offers guided tours, and its location provides some of the most picturesque views in Brittany.
- **Walk the Coastal Path:** Enjoy the GR34 hiking trail along the coast, which offers panoramic views of the cliffs, coves, and pristine beaches of Côtes d'Armor.

Practical Tips:

- Wear comfortable walking shoes and be prepared for windy conditions, especially near the cliffs and coastal areas.
- Bring your camera—the views are stunning, and you'll want to capture the beauty of the coastline.

3. Exploring Paimpol and the Island of Bréhat

- **Distance from Normandy:** Approximately 2 to 2.5 hours by car

- **Why You Should Visit:** Paimpol is a charming coastal town that serves as a gateway to the Island of Bréhat, a car-free island known for its flower-filled gardens, rocky shorelines, and quaint villages.

Things to Do:

- **Paimpol Harbor:** Walk around the harbor of Paimpol, lined with fishing boats, cafés, and shops selling local seafood.
- **Island of Bréhat:** Take a ferry from Paimpol to the Island of Bréhat and explore the flower gardens, lighthouse, and picturesque paths that wind through the island.
- **Visit the Chapel of Saint-Michel:** The chapel sits on a small hill with incredible views of the surrounding sea and coastline.

Practical Tips:

- Ferries to Bréhat Island run regularly from Paimpol, but be sure to check schedules in advance, especially during off-peak seasons.
- Pack a picnic for Bréhat Island, as there are several peaceful spots where you can relax and enjoy the natural beauty.

Normandy for Art Lovers

Normandy has long been a hub for artists—from Impressionists like Claude Monet to modern-day creators—who found inspiration in the region's natural beauty, historical sites, and charming villages. For art lovers, a visit to Normandy is not just about admiring famous artworks, but also about stepping into the creative environments that inspired some of the most influential movements in art history. Explore the picturesque town of Giverny and other artistic retreats that celebrate both Normandy's past and its continuing creative spirit.

1. Giverny – Monet's Dream World

- **Location:** About 1.5 hours from Rouen, accessible by car or train.

- **Why You Should Visit:** Giverny is forever associated with Claude Monet, the father of Impressionism. His stunning gardens and home are a must-visit for anyone interested in art, as they served as the inspiration for some of his most famous paintings, including the Water Lilies series.

Things to Do:

- **Monet's House and Gardens:** Spend time wandering through the beautiful gardens that Monet meticulously designed, including the famous water lily pond, the Japanese bridge, and the vibrant flower gardens. The house itself is a charming abode, filled with personal items and art that give you a sense of Monet's life and creativity.
- **Monet's Paintings:** View Monet's original works at the Musée des Impressionnismes in Giverny, which houses an impressive collection of his paintings and those by his contemporaries.
- **Photography:** Take a walk through the gardens, as the stunning scenery is incredibly photogenic and continues to inspire many artists who visit today.

- **Why You Shouldn't Miss It:** Giverny is a pilgrimage site for art lovers, offering a direct connection to one of the most iconic figures in art history. The peaceful setting of the town and its beautiful gardens make it a perfect retreat for creative souls.

2. Honfleur – A Creative Haven for Artists

- **Location:** Honfleur is located just over an hour from Deauville.

- **Why You Should Visit:** Honfleur has attracted artists for centuries due to its stunning harbor, picturesque old town, and unique light that seems to change the way the landscape is viewed. The town's beauty caught the attention of many Impressionists, including Eugène Boudin and Claude Monet, who both painted scenes of the harbor and seaside views.

Things to Do:

- **Visit the Eugène Boudin Museum:** This museum in Honfleur showcases works by Boudin, one of the pioneers of

Impressionism, along with a collection of Monet's paintings.
- **Explore the Old Port and Streets:** Wander through Honfleur's medieval streets, with its half-timbered houses, art galleries, and local craft shops. Many of the shops sell works by local artists, providing the perfect opportunity to take home a piece of the town's artistic spirit.
- **Le Vieux Bassin:** The old harbor is the heart of Honfleur, and it is surrounded by historic buildings that evoke a sense of timelessness. Artists often set up their easels by the water to capture the stunning reflections of the buildings in the water.

- **Why You Shouldn't Miss It:** Honfleur is an artist's dream, offering both historical inspiration and modern artistic creativity in one charming town. The town's art galleries, historic port, and medieval streets make it a must-see for anyone interested in the arts.

3. Etretat – Inspiration for Landscapes and Seascapes

- **Location:** About 1 hour from Le Havre, along the coast of Normandy.

- **Why You Should Visit:** Known for its dramatic cliffs, rock arches, and beautiful coastline, Etretat has inspired many artists, including Monet and Gustave Courbet. The stunning white chalk cliffs and blue waters of the English Channel create a striking contrast that's perfect for landscape artists.

Things to Do:

- **Cliff Walks:** Take a walk up the cliffs for breathtaking views of the famous rock formations—the Arch and the Needle. These dramatic views have been immortalized in numerous works of art.
- **Visit the Maison de la Nature:** This small museum focuses on nature and the artistic history of Etretat, including the impact of the cliffs on local artists.
- **Etretat Gardens:** Visit the Etretat Gardens on the cliffs, which feature beautifully landscaped areas designed to complement the breathtaking views of the coastline.

- **Why You Shouldn't Miss It:** The cliffs of Etretat are one of the most iconic natural landmarks in France. The region's landscapes have drawn many famous artists, and the town continues to be a haven for creativity.

4. Le Havre – A Modern Art Destination

- **Location:** About 40 minutes from Honfleur.

- **Why You Should Visit:** As a UNESCO World Heritage site, Le Havre is a unique destination for those interested in modern architecture and art. The town's striking design, particularly after its reconstruction following WWII, has made it an important art hub.

Things to Do:

MuMa (Museum of Modern Art): This museum houses a large collection of Impressionist and modern art, including works by Monet, Boudin, and Pissarro.
- **Le Havre's Architecture:** Explore the post-WWII architecture of the town, designed by Auguste Perret, and see how the modern influences have shaped the city's artistic identity.

- **Why You Shouldn't Miss It:** Le Havre offers a unique blend of modern art and historical influence, making it an exciting destination for those interested in art and architecture.

Normandy's natural beauty, historic towns, and creative energy have long inspired artists and continue to attract those looking for a place to nurture their artistic passions. Whether you're exploring Monet's gardens in Giverny, admiring Impressionist paintings in Honfleur, or hiking along the dramatic cliffs of Etretat, Normandy offers a wealth of experiences for art lovers and those eager to connect with their creative spirit.

Conclusion

Reflecting on Your Normandy Journey

As your time in Normandy comes to a close, take a moment to reflect on the rich history, stunning landscapes, and warm hospitality you've experienced. From the majestic cliffs of Etretat to the serene waters of Mont Saint-Michel, Normandy offers a diverse array of experiences that will stay with you long after you've left its shores. Whether you were captivated by the region's medieval towns, moved by the D-Day landmarks, or enchanted by the lush vineyards and charming coastal villages, your journey through Normandy has no doubt created memories to cherish.

Perhaps you've wandered through Bayeux's historic streets, marveled at Monet's water lilies in Giverny, or walked in the footsteps of history at the Normandy beaches. Whether you've explored Normandy's countryside, tasted its world-class cider, or simply enjoyed the peaceful rhythms of life in the region, each moment adds to the story of your Norman adventure.

Here are a few things to remember from your trip:

- **Nature's Beauty:** Normandy's coastal cliffs, verdant gardens, and quaint villages offer a unique and serene connection to nature. From the tide-pool adventures of Mont Saint-Michel to the flower-filled gardens of Giverny, the region's landscapes continue to inspire.

- **Historical Landmarks:** From D-Day's somber memorials to the stunning Norman castles and abbeys, the region offers deep connections to the past. Visiting Omaha Beach, Pegasus Bridge, and the Bayeux Tapestry has undoubtedly given you insight into the legacy of this region.

- **Local Culture and Cuisine:** Normandy's distinctive cuisine, from its cheeses and seafood to its ciders and Calvados, adds layers of flavor to your journey. The region's artistic traditions and vibrant festivals have likely inspired you to appreciate its unique contributions to French culture.

- **Charming Villages and Coastal Beauty:** Whether relaxing in the charming streets of Honfleur, strolling along the beaches of Deauville, or taking in the view from the cliffs of Cap Fréhel, the coastlines and quaint villages have a way of leaving a lasting impression on the heart.

No matter how much you saw, Normandy's beauty has undoubtedly touched your soul in a way that will resonate with you for years to come. The memories you've made here are ones that will keep calling you back, whether in your thoughts, your photographs, or the stories you share with others.

Planning Your Next Adventure in France

Normandy is just one of the many wonderful regions in France that offer diverse experiences waiting to be explored. As your journey in Normandy comes to a close, it's time to think about your next adventure in France. The country is brimming with cultural treasures, beautiful landscapes, and historic sites that will continue to captivate your imagination.

- **Provence – The Heart of the Mediterranean:** If you crave warm

Mediterranean sun, consider heading to Provence. Explore the lavender fields, ancient Roman ruins, and picturesque towns like Aix-en-Provence and Avignon. The food, wine, and stunning landscapes of Provence provide an irresistible appeal.

- **Paris – The City of Light:** No trip to France is complete without experiencing the magic of Paris. Whether you're visiting the Eiffel Tower, strolling through the Louvre, or sipping coffee at a sidewalk café, the City of Light offers endless opportunities to explore art, history, and culture.

- **The French Riviera:** For beaches, luxury resorts, and charming seaside towns, head to the French Riviera. Explore the glamorous lifestyle of Nice, Cannes, and Monaco, and soak up the Mediterranean atmosphere.

- **The Alps:** If you enjoy the mountains, make your way to the French Alps. From Chamonix to Annecy, you'll find hiking, skiing, and an array of outdoor adventures, as well as beautiful lakes, villages, and alpine scenery.

France is an incredibly diverse country, each region offering its own unique charm and experience. From the rolling hills of Normandy to the sun-kissed vineyards of Bordeaux, there is no shortage of adventures to be had.

As you leave Normandy, take with you the spirit of the region—its beauty, its history, its culture, and its warmth. And remember, your next French adventure is only a short distance away. Whether you return to explore more of Normandy or venture into other parts of France, the memories you've created here will remain an important part of your travel story for years to come.

Bon voyage et à bientôt—until your next adventure in France!

Journal

NORMANDY

DATE:

MAIN GOALS FOR THE DAY
(A CLEAR AND CONCISE OBJECTIVE TO GUIDE YOUR PERSONAL GROWTH FOR THE DAY)

TODAY'S MOOD   GOOD ○—○—○—○ NOT GOOD

HOW I TRAVELED

WEATHER

WATER INTAKE   1L   2L   2.5L   3L

BUDGET

TOTAL DAILY BUDGET: $ _____   FOOD & DRINKS: $ _____   ACTIVITIES: $ _____

EXPENSES: $ _____   TRANSPORTATION: $ _____   MISCELLANEOUS: $ _____

PEOPLE I'VE MET

ITINERARY
- MORNING:
- AFTERNOON:
- EVENING:
- NIGHT:

THOUGHTS OF THE DAY
_____
_____

NORMANDY

DATE:

MAIN GOALS FOR THE DAY	TODAY'S MOOD
(A CLEAR AND CONCISE OBJECTIVE TO GUIDE YOUR PERSONAL GROWTH FOR THE DAY)	GOOD — NOT GOOD
	HOW I TRAVELED
	WEATHER
	WATER INTAKE 1L 2L 2.5L 3L

BUDGET

TOTAL DAILY BUDGET: $ _____   FOOD & DRINKS: $ _____   ACTIVITIES: $ _____

EXPENSES: $ _____   TRANSPORTATION: $ _____   MISCELLANEOUS: $ _____

PEOPLE I'VE MET

ITINERARY
- MORNING:
- AFTERNOON:
- EVENING:
- NIGHT:

THOUGHTS OF THE DAY
_____
_____

NORMANDY

DATE:

MAIN GOALS FOR THE DAY	TODAY'S MOOD
(A CLEAR AND CONCISE OBJECTIVE TO GUIDE YOUR PERSONAL GROWTH FOR THE DAY)	○——○——○——○ GOOD NOT GOOD
	HOW I TRAVELED
	WEATHER
	WATER INTAKE 1L 2L 2.5L 3L

BUDGET

TOTAL DAILY BUDGET: $ _____   FOOD & DRINKS: $ _____   ACTIVITIES: $ _____

EXPENSES: $ _____   TRANSPORTATION: $ _____   MISCELLANEOUS: $ _____

PEOPLE I'VE MET

ITINERARY
- MORNING:
- AFTERNOON:
- EVENING:
- NIGHT:

THOUGHTS OF THE DAY

_____

_____

NORMANDY

DATE:

MAIN GOALS FOR THE DAY (A CLEAR AND CONCISE OBJECTIVE TO GUIDE YOUR PERSONAL GROWTH FOR THE DAY)	TODAY'S MOOD	○──○──○──○ GOOD NOT GOOD
	HOW I TRAVELED	✈ 🚆 ❋ ⊖
	WEATHER	☀ ☁ ☁ ☂ ☁ ❋
	WATER INTAKE	💧 💧 💧 💧 1L 2L 2.5L 3L

BUDGET

TOTAL DAILY BUDGET: $ _____   FOOD & DRINKS: $ _____   ACTIVITIES: $ _____

EXPENSES: $ _____   TRANSPORTATION: $ _____   MISCELLANEOUS: $ _____

PEOPLE I'VE MET	ITINERARY
	● MORNING:
	● AFTERNOON:
	● EVENING:
	● NIGHT:

THOUGHTS OF THE DAY

_____

_____

NORMANDY

DATE:

MAIN GOALS FOR THE DAY	TODAY'S MOOD
(A CLEAR AND CONCISE OBJECTIVE TO GUIDE YOUR PERSONAL GROWTH FOR THE DAY)	GOOD — NOT GOOD
	HOW I TRAVELED
	WEATHER
	WATER INTAKE 1L 2L 2.5L 3L

BUDGET

TOTAL DAILY BUDGET: $ _____   FOOD & DRINKS: $ _____   ACTIVITIES: $ _____

EXPENSES: $ _____   TRANSPORTATION: $ _____   MISCELLANEOUS: $ _____

PEOPLE I'VE MET

ITINERARY

- MORNING:
- AFTERNOON:
- EVENING:
- NIGHT:

THOUGHTS OF THE DAY

_____

_____

Word Puzzle

Word Search
Find the hidden words

```
J E X Q K B L N O R M A N D Y
L L S C X E C Q T U G Y T T S
P U K E H X U A V K C P A R Y
T P A C J A K H E W I F P E J
N O I I J W T X T N D F E B J
I M V N Z K G E U R E A S M N
A K M U R I G C A E R N T E M
S R L Q V N O A M U Y J R M M
Q O M E I T T P U K L A Y A E
F N R K E Y E N E U O R B C G
X N I N A K X H O N F L E U R
Y V T S Q U F B A M D K H E J
F I B T J S E H C A E B T K V
N H Z L O E V V R B W Z D P X
W J Y Q X Y A D V O F A F X S
```

D-DAY CIDER CAMEMBERT TAPESTRY
MONT SAINT-MICHEL GIVERNY VIKING COTENTIN
NORMANDY ROUEN HONFLEUR
CAEN BAYEUX CHATEAU BEACHES

Answer

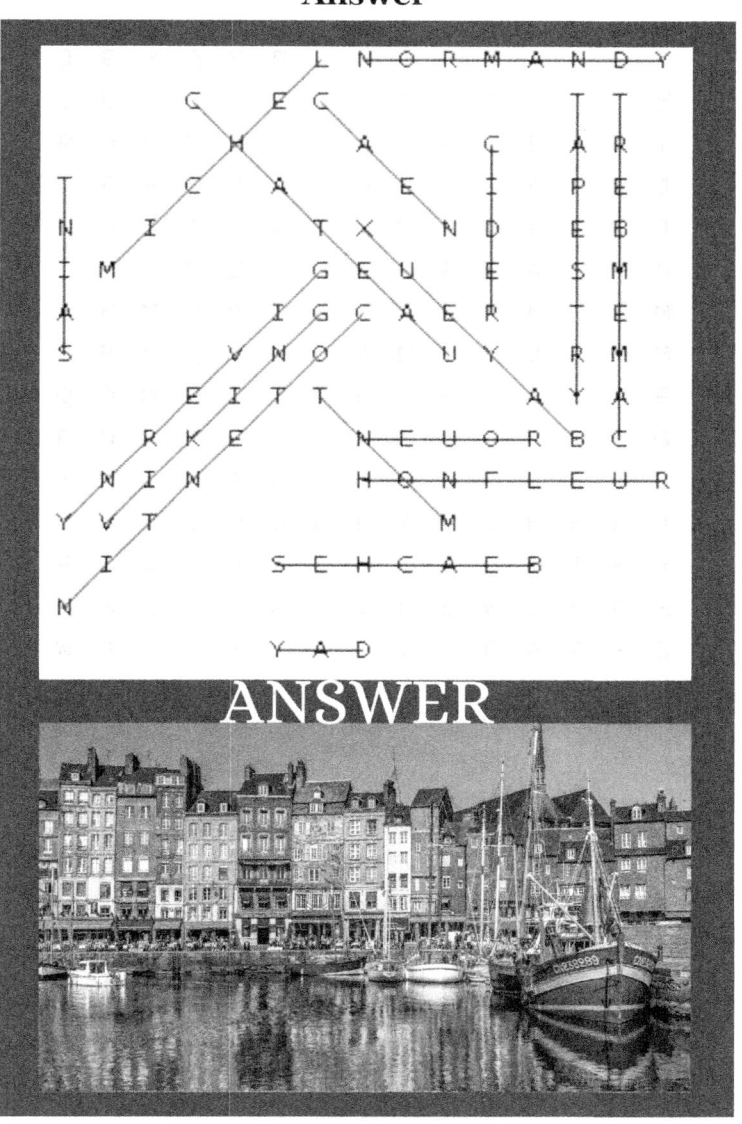

Printed in Dunstable, United Kingdom